THE CHURCH

BY

BARRY CHANT

GENERAL EDITOR KEN CHANT

THE CHURCH

COPYRIGHT © 1988 BY BARRY CHANT

GENERAL EDITOR KEN CHANT

P.O. Box 79,
Werrington NSW 2747, Australia

ISBN: 1-884213-98-7

PUBLISHED BY:
VISION PUBLISHING
940 MONTECITO WAY
RAMONA, CA 92065
(760) 789-4700
WWW.VIU.COM

PRINTED IN THE UNITED STATES OF AMERICA

A Note on Gender

It is unfortunate that the English language does not contain an adequate generic term (especially in the singular number) that includes without bias both male and female. So "he, him, his, man, mankind," with their plurals, must do the work for both sexes. Accordingly, wherever it is appropriate to do so in the following lessons, please include the feminine gender in the masculine, and vice versa.

Footnotes

A work once fully referenced will thereafter be noted throughout the whole series of lessons either by "ibid" or "op. cit."

ABBREVIATIONS

Abbreviations used in the DCC for the books of the Bible are–

OLD TESTAMENT		NEW TESTAMENT
Genesis – Ge	Hosea – Ho	Matthew – Mt
Exodus – Ex	Joel – Jl	Mark – Mk
Leviticus – Le	Amos – Am	Luke – Lu
Numbers – Nu	Obadiah – Ob	John – Jn
Deuteronomy – De	Jonah – Jo	Acts – Ac
Joshua – Jsh	Micah – Mi	Romans – Ro
Judges – Jg	Nahum – Na	1 Corinthians – 1 Co
Ruth – Ru	Habakkuk – Ha	2 Corinthians – 2 Co
1 Samuel – 1 Sa	Zephaniah – Zp	Galatians – Ga
2 Samuel – 2 Sa	Haggai – Hg	Ephesians – Ep
1 Kings – 1 Kg	Zechariah – Zc	Philippians – Ph
2 Kings – 2 Kg	Malachi – Mal	Colossians – Cl
1 Chronicles – 1 Ch		1 Thessalonians – 1 Th
2 Chronicles – 2 Ch		2 Thessalonians – 2 Th
Ezra – Ezr		1 Timothy – 1 Ti
Nehemiah – Ne		2 Timothy – 2 Ti
Esther – Es		Titus – Tit
Job – Jb		Philemon – Phm
Psalms – Ps		Hebrews – He
Proverbs – Pr		James – Ja
Ecclesiastes – Ec		1 Peter – 1 Pe
Song of Solomon – Ca*		2 Peter – 2 Pe
Isaiah – Is		1 John – 1 Jn
Jeremiah – Je		2 John – 2 Jn
Lamentations – La		3 John – 3 Jn
Ezekiel – Ez		Jude – Ju
Daniel – Da		Revelation – Re

* *Ca* is an abbreviation of *Canticles*, a derivative of the Latin name of the *Song of Solomon*, which is sometimes also called the *Song of Songs*.

Preface

An Invincible Church

by Ken Chant

Jesus said: *"I will build my church, and the gates of hell will not prevail against it"* (Mt 16:18).

That saying comes strangely to our ears – we do not usually think of *gates* as *prevailing* – but to the people of Bible days it was pregnant with meaning. In fact, Jesus' words must have had a stunning impact on his hearers.

The phase *"the gates of hell"* was a common idiom in the Greek world. It was used to convey the idea of the strongest possible force. Today we might say, *"mighty as an atom bomb... powerful as an earthquake... terrible as a tornado;"* but when a Greek wanted to express irresistible, invincible force, he would speak about *"the gates of hell"* – he could think of nothing stronger.

Now to people who were familiar with that idiom, the effect of associating it with Jesus' little band of disciples must have been quite startling. As though he had said –

> *"Until now you have known nothing mightier than the gates of hell – but I am about to create a new thing, my church, against which the gates of hell will be as impotent as a paper sword against granite!"*

What does this mean to us?

The Church is the Toughest Thing on Earth

The church tough? Indestructible?

On the face of it that proposition would seem absurd to many people even today; but it must have seemed still more absurd to the people who first heard Jesus proclaim it.

Look at the scene: Jesus is speaking to a small collection of fishermen, tax collectors, publicans, and peasants – only a dozen men all told, and one of them is under suspicion of being a thief. Yet Christ is promising to turn them into a body tougher than the proverbial *"gates of hell."* One can almost hear a guffaw of derision: *"What? That lot? Tougher than hell? It'll be a wonder if they survive the first prod of a Roman spear!"*

Even the men Jesus was speaking to found it hard to accept. In fact, neither they nor anyone else was surprised when, some two years later, he was arrested in Jerusalem and they *did* all desert him (Mt 26:56).

But God gathered them together again, poured out his Spirit upon them (Ac 2:1-4), put steel in their courage, and began to build the church that across the centuries has indeed proved itself to be the toughest thing on earth!

Despite two millennia of conflict - through rivers of blood, against fire and sword, rack and lash and prison, fang and claw, hatred, slander, and falsehood - the church has stood firm.

Gloriously, incredibly, the promise of Christ has proved to be absolutely true. Against his church, not even the gates of hell have been able to prevail!

As the old historian Eusebius wrote -

"Words cannot describe the outrageous agonies endured by the martyrs ... They were torn to bits from head to foot with potsherds like claws till death released them. Women were bound by one foot and hoisted high in the air by machines, head downwards, and with their bodies completely naked, without a morsel of clothing, thus presenting to all onlookers a most shameful, brutal, and inhuman spectacle. Others were tied to the branches and trunks of trees, and died horribly; for with the aid of machinery, the persecutors drew together the stoutest boughs, fastened the limbs of the martyrs to them, and then let the boughs fly back to their normal positions - thus they instantly tore apart the bodies of their victims. In this way they carried on - not for a few days or weeks, but year after year ... (There were occasions) when during a single day a hundred men, as well as women and little children were killed, after being subjected to a succession of ever-changing torments ... (They were) torn apart with hooks, broken on the rack, mercilessly flogged, subjected to countless other tortures too terrible to describe, in endless variety, until they were finally given to the flames ... (Some) died under the torture itself, others were starved to death ... (But always they showed) a most wonderful ardor, the kind of truly divine energy and zeal that belongs to those who believe in the Christ of God. For as soon as sentence was pronounced against (one martyr), another and still another would rush to the judgment seat and confess that they were Christians. They regarded with indifference the terrible cruelty, and the many different tortures, and with undaunted boldness declared their devotion to the God of the universe. They received the final sentence of death with joy, laughter, and gaiety. Until their very last breath they sang, offering up hymns of thanksgiving to the God of the universe ..." [1]

So, for each martyr who fell, a hundred more sprang to take his place, until the church, invincible, went on to girdle the earth!

Yet now, despite this record, and despite the continuing heroism of the martyr church behind the Iron Curtain, the promise of Christ is once again being scorned.

In our society men are describing the church as a fusty anachronism; they talk of the "post-Christian" era; they equate the church with a dithering and effeminate parson; they picture it as a sweet old lady in a rocking chair - redundant as an ice- box in Iceland, harmless as a toothless teddy bear, obsolete as a stage coach on a freeway.

The church an image of toughness? The idea is a joke to many people. But behind the facade of denominationalism there still remains the real church of Jesus Christ, the one that he is building. That real church, that inner core of committed people, will prove today and in the future to be as unconquerable and as triumphant as it has been in the past. As S. Baring-Gould sang in *Onward Christian Soldiers*! -

> *Crowns and thrones may perish.*
>
> *Kingdoms rise and wane,*

---

[1] *Church History*, Bk. VIII, ch 9, ff. The above, of course, is only a small selection from the extensive accounts of the martyrs given by Eusebius.

But the church of Jesus
Constant will remain;
Gates of hell can never
'Gainst that church prevail;
We have Christ's own promise -
And that cannot fail!

In that tough church, the toughest thing on earth, the insecure find unshakable security, the nameless find divine identity, the lonely find unfailing fellowship, the dying find indestructible life, the disgraced find endless glory. All who yearn for those treasures had better get into that church! (He 12:22-24).

THE CHURCH IS UNHARMED BY DEATH

In modern English the word *hell*, has come to mean the place of fiery torment where the damned will suffer for eternity. That was not its original meaning in English, nor did the Greek word used by Matthew hold that primary meaning. The Greek word is *hades*, which means simply *"the abode of the dead."* That was also the earliest meaning of the old Anglo-Saxon word *hell*, or *hel*.

In Greek mythology *hades* was pictured as a deep gloomy cavern in the bowels of the earth (or sometimes of the sea). It was a place quite distinct from the grave. When a person died, said the Greeks, his body was buried in the grave, but his *shade* (his ghostly self) traveled down into the nether world, into *hades*.

Actually, *"Hades"* was the personal name of the god who was supposed to preside over that grim and shadowy haunt, a god so fearsome, so powerful, that the Greeks became terrified of even pronouncing his name. So they called him Pluto, *The Wealthy One*, because he owned all of earth's precious metals and deep-buried jewels. This Pluto was served by the *Furies* - gruesome female sub-deities who had heads like dogs, snake-entwined hair, pitch-black bodies, awful blood- dripping eyes, and who carried brass-studded thongs to scourge the guilty dead.

Once the pitiless gates of hades had closed behind a *shade*, it was believed that not even the chief of the gods, Zeus, could rescue the unhappy captive from the relentless hands of Pluto and his Furies. From that dread and dark imprisonment there was no escape. So the phrase *"the gates of hades,"* became synonymous with the merciless and unbreakable power of death.

But Christ seized the old Greek myth and made it an image of the victory he would give his church. As though he had said -

> *"Even if you should die and be plunged to the very bottom of hades, yet if you belong to my church you cannot be held there! Those gates will be torn off their hinges as though they were twigs. You will rise again! Death cannot chain you!"*

Our trail-blazer has become Jesus, who himself conquered death. As Peter shouted to the people in Jerusalem -

> *"We speak of the resurrection of Christ, that he was not abandoned in hades, nor did his flesh see corruption ... God raised him up, and of that we are all witnesses"* (Ac 2:25-32).

If it is asked how we can be sure the ancient testimony is true, we reply that we have at least two infallible witnesses that Jesus is alive today -

<u>His Name</u>: the name of a *dead*, man could not do what the name of Jesus does - heal the sick, cast out demons, meet financial needs, hush storms, open prison doors, smash sin, move mountains, change the world!

His name has power because his living, personal presence goes along with his name. If he should die, his name would become as futile against the raging powers of darkness as any other. But because he lives, all of his wealth and divine power is vested in his name, JESUS!

<u>His Spirit</u>: he could not give the Holy Spirit in glory and power, and with supernatural signs, unless he were *alive* and sitting with authority in the heavenlies (Ac 2:1-4, 32-33).

Every time I speak in tongues, with the rivers of joy coursing through my soul, I hear the sound of the black gates of hell being crushed, the sound of the great stone being rolled away (Mt 28:2), and I know that Jesus is alive for ever!

That glossolalic sound is like the rattling Ezekiel heard when the breath of the Spirit swept across his valley of dry bones, and behold, the bones came together, and flesh formed on them, and they stood up, a mighty host, alive from the dead! (Ez 37:7-10). It is the sound of resurrection! It is the witness of heaven that we who believe in Jesus will share his marvellous conquest of the grave. Death cannot grip us any better than it could grip him because, like him, we are quickened by the eternal Spirit (Ro 8:11).

To every person who is built into the church that Christ is building, *"the gates of hell"* have become rather the gates of everlasting life!

THE CHURCH DOMINATES SATAN

In Bible days governors, councilors, judges, often held court near the gates of a city; hence, by a process called metonymy, *gates* became synonymous with *government* or *authority*. The same process occurs today when we say *Washington* instead of *"the federal government of the USA,"* or *London* instead of *"the national parliament of Great Britain."*

So we use the name of one thing to describe another with which it is associated in some way.

Hence, *"the gates of Jerusalem,"* or *"the gates of Jericho,"* in Bible days, was a convenient and colorful way of describing the civic or legal authorities that ruled in those cities.

In the same way, the phrase *"the gates of Hell,"* conveyed to Jesus' hearers the idea of the *kingdom*, of darkness, and of its ruling sovereign, Satan. Christ was saying that although the devil and his legions may storm out of the gates of the diabolic kingdom, and may fall with furious hatred upon the church, their onslaughts will be in vain. It is easier to shift a mountain with a feather than to overturn his church!

Paul had the same idea when he wrote -

"God has delivered us from the dominion of darkness and transferred us to the kingdom of his beloved Son;"

and again -

"We are not contending against flesh and blood, but against the principalities, against the powers, against the world rulers of this present darkness, against the spiritual hosts of wickedness in the heavenly places ... (and our) weapons are mighty through God to pull down the strongholds (of Satan)" (Cl 2:13; Ep 6:12; 2 Co 10:3-4).

Christ has given us authority to crush our enemy ruthlessly beneath our feet (Lu 10:17-20; also see Ro 16:20). No matter how cunning Satan's plans, nor how wicked his designs, nor how dreadful his power, nor how immense his resources, his efforts will all finally be vain. He neither can destroy the church as a whole, nor even one congregation that stands firm in Christ. The church will prevail, and continue to advance from glory to glory, long after the gates of hell have decayed into dust!

Here then is the secret of personal triumph. The logic is irrefragable: *those who belong to an invincible church will themselves be invincible.* And the more closely you are bound to the church, the more you will share in its divine strength.

Spiritual health, spiritual power, personal fulfillment, mastery over Satan - all of these arise from close fellowship with the church of Jesus Christ, and from active participation in its worship, and in its witness.

But notice that the promise of Christ is only this: *"the gates of hell"* cannot prevail against the church that <u>he</u> is building. Any other church - whether a particular denomination, or a particular local assembly - may fall, if it has ceased to be a true expression of the church of Jesus, or if it never was built by him. But so long as Christ has cause to identify a congregation as a valid part of that true church he himself is building, then it will remain a fact: *against that church, and against those who are a vital part of it, the gates of hell can never prevail.*

The task my brother Barry has attempted in these lessons is to describe the church that Christ is building, a church that has scant respect for either national or denominational barriers, a church that reflects the spirit and character that was born on the day of Pentecost. But I will let him explain his theme in his own introduction (which follows immediately).

My part in this book has been to edit the whole (so I will take the blame for any errors it may contain) and to write this introductory chapter.

Neither Barry nor I are waving a flag for any particular denomination. We find both wheat and tares in all parts of the church. But we have tried, as fairly as we can, to show you the picture that the N.T. gives of the church, for we believe that only those churches that do reflect N.T. principles will succeed in fulfilling the mandate of Christ.

May the Lord of the church give you pleasure and instruction as you study these pages.

TABLE OF CONTENTS

Author's *Introduction.*

Various Greek words examined: people, city, herald, crowd, synagogue, and church (*ekklesia*) – the use of *ekklesia* in the N.T., to describe the universal church and the local church.

The nature of the local church – visible or invisible? – its name – how big it should be – various meeting places – Paul likens the church to the human body.

Continuing the last chapter, various other analogies of the church: a temple, a household, a lampstand, a field, a vine, a bride, a flock, an army.

The difference between descriptive and prescriptive passages – the nature of ascension-gift ministries – the five ministries: *apostles, prophet, evangelist, pastor, teacher* – the ministry of an *apostle*: its nature, extent, and limitations – the ministry of the *prophet*: in the O.T. and the N.T., its nature, extent, and limitations.

The ministry of an *evangelist* – the example of Philip – the *evangel* – the ministry of a *pastor* – the example of Jesus – the qualifications, duties, and limits of pastoral ministry – the ministry of a *teacher* – its importance and function in the church – the example of Jesus and of Apollos.

Ministry gifts and natural gifts – a general summary – the ministries of Timothy and Titus.

The three systems of government: *Episcopal, Congregational, and Presbyterian* – membership in the local church.

The meaning of "elder," "bishop," and "pastor" – historical background of "elder" – a plural or single eldership? – how the episcopal system developed – the duties of elders.

The relationship between local church leaders and other ministry gifts – apostolic authority – pastoral authority – balanced authority – summary.

Inter-church organization: by location, by apostolic integration, by fraternal interest, by historical develpments – conclusions – a paradigm of autonomous local churches.

The principles governing appointment to office – how apostles were appointed – the appointment of elders and deacons.

A revelation of the family as a paradigm of the church – definition of a family – apostles and the churches as a family – the roles of "father," "grandfather," and "son" – prophets, evangelists, pastors, teachers, and the churches as a family.

The church as a worshiping family of faith – worship in the N.T. church – the "mystery" religions – the synagogue – worship in the first and second centuries – summary.

"Fellowship" in the early church – the meaning of *koinonia*: partnership and sharing – analogies of "fellowship," its practice.

CHAPTER EIGHT

Discipline in the N.T. church – the nature and scope of discipline – the standards of holiness and truth – the corporate and personal aim of discipline – the practice of discipline – the correct procedure.

The ministry of women in the church: their role and authority.

CHAPTER NINE

A study of giving in the O.T. and in the N.T. – the tithe was the O.T. basis of giving – the various tithes and who received them – the purpose of tithing in the O.T. – the nature of Christian giving – two basic principles: obedience and faith – the law of sowing and reaping.

The sacraments – how the idea of "mystery" developed into "sacrament" – are the sacraments means of grace, or merely symbols? – the word of God (not sacraments) lies at the heart of the church – a balanced approach to the sacraments – how many sacraments? – in what sense can they be a means of grace?

CHAPTER TEN

The three major elements in planting new churches are *Message* (the proclamation of the evangel); *Method* (gifted ministries bearing witness of Christ in all kinds of places, to small and large groups, in the power of the Holy Spirit, in the name of Jesus, with faith); *Marketing* (through preaching and teaching, with miracles, by the power of the Holy Spirit, and despite persecution).

The nature of the kingdom – definition of terms used in the N.T. – an invisible kingdom – entry into the kingdom – its final establishment – the kingdom parables – the difference between the church and the kingdom – the one is visible and divisible; the other is invisible and indivisible – conclusion and bibliography.

CHAPTER ONE

WHAT IS THE CHURCH?

INTRODUCTION

One of my favorite cartoons (drawn by John Lawing) [2] shows a senior demon talking to his friend. In the background is a church building from which are coming obvious signs of violent argument and dispute. *"We always start the juniors on church politics,"* says the older demon. *"Never fails!"*

There is more than a little truth in this! Churches have probably argued about politics (that is, leadership structure, buildings and equipment, constitutions, fiscal policies, and so on) as much as anything else.

My purpose in writing this book is not to become another of those quarrelsome voices, but simply to show how churches functioned in New Testament days. My emphasis will not be on organization, but on the example set by the early church evangelistically, pastorally, apostolically, spiritually.

Indeed, when we get down to basics, the kind of organization a church adopts is probably the least vital factor of all. Some formal structures, of course, must exist, for without them no church could function. There are also a number of structural models that churches can adopt - some more successful than others.

But the fact remains that most New Testament principles of church life can be applied within any good organizational pattern. So while I shall give some attention to organization, my main focus will be on the church itself, how it worshipped, evangelized, taught, grew, fellowshipped, and so on.

If we can catch something of the spirit of the New Testament church today, we shall be well on the way to seeing a major extension of the kingdom of God in our land.

---

[2] Famous for his *"What If..."* cartoons that appeared for many years in *"Christianity Today."*

SOME STRANGE OPINIONS

A group of young people were once asked to describe the picture that came into their minds when they heard the word *"church."* Here are some of their replies -

> *"ancient grey building, ceremonies, robes, candles"*
>
> *"dithering, unmanly, sentimental, weak"*
>
> *"a place of charity, welfare, helping the poor"*
>
> *"a place of learning, a kind of school"*
>
> *"where people find God and learn how to pray"*
>
> *"long sermons, a big bore, a waste of time"*
>
> *"people who think they are better than anyone else"* [3]

Plainly, those young people had a distorted image of the church and little idea of what it really is and how it functions.

But there are also many people who love the church, yet who are scarcely more able to say what it is. They have only a vague notion of what the New Testament teaches. So we will begin at the very beginning, that is, with the word church itself.

In everyday speech, *church* is used with a number of different meanings. List here as many of those meanings as you can -

________________________   ________________________

________________________   ________________________

________________________   ________________________

________________________   ________________________

In New Testament days, of course, some of those meanings did not apply (for example, building, denomination, hierarchy). The Greek word for *church (ekklesia)* had a narrower meaning than the English word. However, before we can define that Greek word, we need to look at its history and compare it with some other common words. By doing this we can discover just what *ekklesia* meant to the people who used it back in Bible days.

---

[3] Adapted from a random survey taken by a pastor who is a friend of mine.

1.   "EKKLESIA" IN THE GREEK WORLD

1.1   PEOPLE

Greek: *demos*

Originally this word meant a divided territory or district, but later came to be used of the people who inhabit a particular land or city -

> *"It can have the derogatory nuance of the mob as distinct from the aristocracy. But it can also have a proud ring, as in Athens, where it is used for the free and self-governing citizens."* [4]

Demos is used four times in the New Testament, signifying the populations of *Jerusalem* (Ac 12:22), *Thessalonica* (17:5), and *Ephesus* (19:30, 33).

1.2   CITY

Greek: *polis*

The *polis* was originally a city-state, that is, an independent state made up of a city and the surrounding territory directly controlled by it. By New Testament days *polis* was being used mostly of a city itself - its buildings, streets, walls (Mt 2:23; 5:14; 8:33; etc.) - but it could also be used of the people who lived there, just as we use the word today (for example, Ac 13:44; 14:21; 19:29).

Polis occurs 159 times in the New Testament.

1.3   HERALD

Greek: *kerux*

The function of a herald varied over the centuries; but his normal task was to deliver a proclamation on behalf of someone in authority, or to call an assembly together -

> *"He at once sent the heralds to call the people to assembly. So they called them and the people together..."* [5]

---

[4] Kittel, *Theological Dictionary of the New Testament*, Vol. 2, pg. 63; Eerdmans Pub. Co., Grand Rapids, Michigan; 1964.
[5] Homer, *The Iliad*, II. 7ff. See Brown, *Dictionary of New Testament Theology*, Vol. 3, pg. 48ff; Zondervan Publishing House, Grand Rapids, Michigan; 1971.

Although *kerux* occurs only four times in the New Testament, the derivative word *kerygma* (preaching) occurs eight times (1 Co 1:18, 21; etc.), and the verb kerusso ("I preach") occurs 61 times.

1.4   CROWD

Greek: *ochlos*

This word simply means a large group of people, usually gathered spontaneously, and without organization. It is the word translated in the Authorized Version as *multitude* (79 times) or *people* (32 times). It occurs in the New Testament 174 times.

1.5   SYNAGOGUE

Greek: *sunagoge*

This word means literally "gathering together." It was frequently used in the LXX to describe the assembly or congregation of Israel, especially in a religious setting.

By New Testament days it had come to be used of

> "either the meeting place of the local Jewish community or the congregation itself ... since the assembly most often took place in the synagogue building, the word carried both meanings." [6]

There were evidently several synagogues in Jerusalem, representing different countries of origin (cp. Ac 6:9). Only in James 2:2 is the word used of a Christian gathering. It was probably avoided by most Christians because the synagogue had come to be a symbol of Jewish law and tradition (this is obvious from the New Testament - Mt 23:2; Ac 15:21; etc.)

Sunagoge was also used in New Testament days to describe the festive assemblies of some Greek cultic associations or guilds. [7]

1.6   CHURCH

Greek: *ekklesia*

This word was used in pre-Christian times to denote a meeting of all the citizens of a city (*polis*). It derives from the verb *kaleo* ("I call"). It

---

[6] Ibid. Vol. 1, pg. 296ff.
[7] Ibid, pg. 292.

denotes a calling out (*ex* = out, plus *klesis* = call, or invitation); but this *calling out* was actually for the purpose of a *calling together*, that is, for a meeting.

The use of *ekklesia* to describe a gathering of all citizens reached its greatest importance in the 5th century BC, when the *ekklesia* met regularly to govern the affairs of the city-state (for example, in Athens it met 30 to 40 times a year).

Originally, only men of certain economic status were permitted to attend (for example, men whose wealth was not less than the value of "500 bushels"); but later admission to the *ekklesia* became more timocratic (that is, based on honor and standing more than on property ownership, and the like) and all full citizens were accepted. Nonetheless, attendance at the *ekklesia* was permitted only to men. No women were allowed.

The *ekklesia* dealt with such matters as appointments to official positions, changes of the law, internal and external policy, disputes that required special judgment. It normally opened with prayers and sacrifices to the gods. Any citizen could propose matters for discussion, but such matters could only be dealt with when there was expert opinion present. Decisions were reached by voting, whether by show of hands, ballot sheets or stones, or by voices. [8]

The important thing to note is that there was a clear distinction between the people (*demos*) and/or the city (*polis*) on the one hand, and the assembly (*ekklesia*) on the other.

As one writer puts it -

" ... from the time of Thucidides, Plato, and Xenophon, ekklesia is the assembly of the *demos* in Athens and in most Greek *poleis*. The etymology is both simple and significant. The citizens are the *ekkletoi*, that is, those who are summoned and called together by the kerux." [9]

It is clear, then, that *ekklesia* was used to describe an actual meeting together of certain citizens, especially when those citizens had been called together by the herald into a formal assembly.

---

[8] Ibid, pg. 291.
[9] Kittel, Vol. 3, pg. 513ff.

1.7 SUMMARY

When we consider the meaning of *ekklesia* we must first understand its common use in the secular world of New Testament times. While everybody made up either the people (*demos*), or the city (*polis*), only full citizens who were summoned by a herald (*kerux*) belonged to the *ekklesia*. In other words, it was possible to be one of the people without being a member of the assembly (*ekklesia*). Furthermore, the assembly existed only when it was actually meeting. Until the qualified citizens gathered formally, there was no *ekklesia*.

2. "EKKLESIA" IN THE NEW TESTAMENT

Ekklesia occurs in the New Testament 115 times. Those occurrences can be analyzed as follows -

The Universal Church	12 times
The Local Church	60 times
Local Churches	35 times
Other Usage	28 times

There are four references where either the local or the universal church may be intended (1 Co 10:32; 15:9; Ga 1:13; Ph 3:6). When Paul, for example, said that he had *"persecuted the church of God"* he may have been referring to the whole church, or just to the church in Jerusalem. (The use of the word *"church"* rather than, say, *"saints,"* also suggests that Christians were arrested while they were actually meeting together as a church.)

There are a further four places where *ekklesia* does not refer to the Christian church at all (Ac 7:38; 19:32, 39, 41).

It is also interesting to note that *ekklesia* occurs only three times in the gospels (Mt 16:18; 18:17), and that only one of those is a clear reference to the Christian church. Luke, for instance, employs the term frequently in Acts, but never in his gospel. Obviously the church is seen as being a post-Pentecost phenomenon.

2.1 THE UNIVERSAL CHURCH

The concept of a universal church - that is, a world-wide body of all believers - is far more common today than it was in New Testament days.

Hence the New Testament writers usually preferred to talk about *"the churches"* rather than *"the church."*

So Paul speaks of *"the churches of Galatia"* (Ga 1:2), or *"the churches of Asia"* (1 Co 16:19), or *"the churches of God"* (1 Co 11:16). An exception is found in Acts 9:31, where *ekklesia* in the Greek text is singular (not plural, as indicated in the Authorized Version). Paul's usual style was followed by the other apostles. Hence John, for example, spoke of *"the seven churches in Asia"* (Re 1:11, 20).

Nevertheless, the New Testament gives clear evidence that among those early churches there was a continuing and developing sense of unity, of viewing the group of churches as one body. This was no doubt an inevitable consequence of

- the increasing number of both believers and churches in the world. [10]

- the increasing number of believers who had died.

So in Paul's later letters, such as Ephesians and Colossians, a wider view of the church is evident. It is not merely a local congregation, but rather the whole body of people, both living and dead, who acknowledge one Head, Jesus Christ. This greater Church is universal in time as well as space (compare He 12:23).

When Paul says that Christ is head over all things, including the church which is his body (Ep 1:22 ff), there can hardly be any doubt that he is talking about the whole church. The same idea is evident in 3:10, 21; 5:25-27; and Cl 1:18. Christ certainly died for the whole church (5:25),

---

[10] For example, late in the second century, Tertullian was able to write in protest against those who were persecuting the church -

"If we desired indeed to act the part of open enemies (of the Roman authorities) ... would there be any lacking in (our) strength, whether of numbers or resources? ... We are but of yesterday, (yet) we have filled every place among you - cities, islands, fortresses, towns, market-places, the very camp, tribes, companies, palace, senate, forum - we have left nothing to you but the temples of your gods ... (What) if such multitudes of men were to break away from you, and betake themselves to some remote corner of the world, why the very loss of so many citizens, whatever sort they were, would cover the empire with shame ... Why, you would be horror struck at the solitude in which you would find yoursevles, at such an all-prevailing silence, and that stupor as of a dead world. You would have to seek subjects to govern. You would have more enemies than citizens remaining. For now it is the immense numbers of Christians which makes your enemies so few - almost all the inhabitants of your various cities being followers of Christ!" (*Apology*, ch. 37; *The Ante-Nicene Fathers*, Vol. 3, pg. 45; Eerdmans Pub. Co. Grand Rapids, Michigan; 1978 reprint.)

not for just a part of it. This is the church that Jesus said he himself would build (Mt 16:18).

Unity is a major thrust of the idea that the church is Christ's *"body"* (Ep 1:23). There is but one body, just as there is but one Spirit, one Lord, one faith, one baptism, and one God and Father of all (4:4-6). Hence, all who honor that one God, through the one Lord Jesus Christ and the one Holy Spirit, are themselves essentially one - they are members of one church, one great assembly of people called together under one name.

That is why Peter, although he does not in fact use the word *ekklesia*, does describe *"God's elect, strangers in the world, scattered throughout Pontius, Galatia, Cappadocia, Asia and Bithynia"* (1:1), as *"a chosen people, a royal priesthood, a holy nation, a people belonging to God ..."* (2:9) - that is, as one group of people.

The New Testament, therefore, recognizes two formations of the church, and no other: there is the church universal; and there are local churches. The only recognizable grouping of churches is geographic: the churches of *Asia* (1 Co 16:19), of *Galatia* (Ga 1:2), of *Macedonia* (2 Co 8:1); etc. Otherwise they are simply known as the *"churches of Christ"* (Ro 61;16), or *"of God"* (1 Co 11:16). But this geographic grouping, or organizing, of local churches was done for mostly practical purposes, usually under the influence of an apostle or similar leader (2 Co 8:1 ff; 9:1 ff; 1 Co 16:1 ff; Ph 4:14 ff). Denominations as we know them today were unknown, and any suggestion of them was normally condemned (1 Co 1:10 ff).

> * **Think Spot**: *Does your local church belong to a larger group of organized churches? If so, on what basis is the group organized: geographical, doctrinal, practical, cultural, historical, ethical, fraternal?*

Many churches belong to denominations that are spread across the entire nation. Yet it is really impossible for people in one State to have any significant fellowship with those in another distant State. How much easier it would be to have fellowship with people in your own State who, although belonging to different denominations, are of similar persuasion. Would it not be better - and more scriptural - for all the people in one region to be recognized as *"the churches of that region,"* rather than by denomination?

How difficult would it be to implement this? If you think it would be very difficult, ask yourself why?

Is there a valid place for denominations? If not, why not?

2.2 A LOCAL ASSEMBLY

As we have seen, the *ekklesia* is basically a local assembly of people. The simplest way to establish that in the New Testament this is the dominant idea of the church, is to read the word "*assembly*," or even better "*meeting*" or "*congregation*," whenever the word "*church*" appears. If you can do this successfully, then the local church is intended. And in fact you will be able to do it in the majority of cases. The clear emphasis in the New Testament is on local assemblies, that is, on the actual meeting together of Christians to form an *ekklesia.*

The term *ekklesia* was primarily applied either to the meeting itself, or to the group of people who attended the meeting. As far as the New Testament is concerned, no one could be a member of a local church who was not actually and actively present at the meetings of that church. [11]

3. THE LOCAL CHURCH

From a study of the New Testament, we can learn what local churches were like in New Testament days. This helps us to answer important questions about what churches should be like today.

3.1 WHAT IS THE RELATIONSHIP BETWEEN LOCAL CHURCHES AND THE UNIVERSAL CHURCH?

The local church is a microcosm of the universal church. It is not *part* of the Church of God - it *is* the Church of God. The language of the New Testament suggests that everything the universal church is may be found in the local church.

For example, in his greetings to the Corinthian church, Paul calls it "*the Church of God in Corinth*" (1 Co 1:2; 2 Co 1:1) - that is, in every respect it *is* God's church.

That is why the New Testament uses similar language to describe both the local and universal expressions of the church. Consider 1 Timothy

---

[11] Allowance was of course made for extraordinary circumstances, such as imprisonment, war service, extended illness, and the like.

3:15. The second half of the verse appears universal in its scope; but the first half clearly refers to the local church. Similarly, 1 Corinthians 12:28 is frequently taken to refer to the universal church, yet (as the context clearly shows) it is actually a reference to the local church (see below, 4:1, "*The church as a body*").

---

* **Think Spot**: *Does this mean that every local church should have its own apostles, prophets, etc.?*

In the light of this, consider some New Testament local churches: Antioch *(Ac 13:1 ff);* Rome *(Ro 16:1 ff);* Corinth *(1 Co 12:1 ff); etc.*

Certainly there is a profound challenge here.

3.2   IS THE TRUE CHURCH VISIBLE OR INVISIBLE?

Remember that the 5th century Greek *ekklesia* was an actual assembly of citizens. The New Testament *ekklesia* was similar. It was an actual meeting. See 1 Co 11:18, which reads literally, "*when you assemble <u>as</u> a church*" (not, "<u>*in*</u> *the church*").

Compare also the use of the word in Acts 19. First, the city (*polis*) is in an uproar (vs. 29). Then the people (*demos*) seize Paul's companions and rush to the theatre (vs. 29-30, 33). Once there, they become an assembly (*ekklesia*, vs. 32) although so disorganized that the word "*crowd*" (*ochlos*) is also used to describe them (vs. 33, 35). Later, the city clerk suggests they should settle the matter in a properly constituted assembly (*ekklesia*, vs. 39) and dismisses the assembly (*ekklesia*) in question (vs. 41).

Notice that the crowd is addressed as an *ekklesia* only when it is actually gathered together. In the same way the church, too, is really only a church when it is actually gathered together. William Tyndale, in his 16th century English translation of the New Testament, showed that he understood this idea, by commonly translating *ekklesia* as "*congregation*" (not "*church*").

---

* **Think Spot**: *Is it, then, possible to be a Christian without being actively involved in a local church?*

The concept of the *invisible* church is largely a Reformation one, [12] although it was first developed by Augustine in *The City of God.* [13] In Reformation theology the church was described in *"spiritual"* terms as consisting solely of true believers in Christ. By contrast, in the New Testament the possibility of hypocrites being in the church is recognized - that is, not all who appear to be of the church really are. Only the Lord knows those who are truly his (2 Ti 2:19; cp. Ro 9:6 ff). The parables of the wheat and the weeds (Mt 13:24-43) and the sheep and the goats (Mt 25:31-46) also illustrate this point. Those scriptures are meaningful only on the presumption that the church is primarily a visible company of people on earth.

So the *"invisible"* church arises out of, and depends on, the *"visible"* church (not vice versa). The only way to belong to that *invisible* church is first to belong to the *visible* one - and that means belonging to a local church, for that is the only visible form of the church.

3.3   How Should Local Churches Be Identified?

In the New Testament local churches are described as being:

"of God:"	- twelve times (Ac 12:5; 20:28; 1 Co 1:2; 10:32; 11:16, 22; 15:9; 1 Co 1:1; 1 Th 2:14; 2 Th 1:4; 1 Ti 3:5, 15).
"of Christ:"	- once (Ro 16:16; but see also 1 Th 2:14; Mt 16:18; Ep 1:23;1 Co 12:27).
"of the saints:"	- once (1 Co 14:33).

---

[12] See Calvin's *Institutes of theChristian Religion,* IV.1.7.

[13] Throughout *The City of God* Augustine thinks of the church as the total body of believers on the earth, at war with the equally universal City of the World. He referred to the universal church in other writings also -

"... we are here to understand the whole Church, not that part of it only which wanders as a stranger on the earth, praising the name of God from the rising of the sun to the going down of the same ... but that part also which has always from its creation remained steadfast to God in heaven, and has never experienced the misery consequent upon a fall. This part is made up of the holy angels..." (*Enchiridion*, ch 56).

"... this name is the holy church, the one church, the true church, the catholic (universal) church, fighting against all heresies: fight, it can; be brought down, it cannot" (*On the Creed*, 14).

"... the universal church, of which (all pious widows) are members..." (*On the Good of Widowhood*, 14). *The Nicene Fathers, First Series*, Vol. 2; Eerdmans reprint, 1979.

Otherwise churches are identified by location. See the titles of each of Paul's letters: see also 1 Co 16:1, 19; 2 Co 8:1; Ga 1:2; 1 Th 1:1; Cl 4:16; etc. This regional identification may be further narrowed into the actual location of the meeting place - for example, Priscilla and Aquila had churches in their two homes, in *Ephesus* (Ac 18:26; 1 Co 16:19) and *Rome* (Ro 16:5). So, too, did Nympha, in *Laodicea* (Cl 4:15).

Meetings identified by the names of their leaders (and presumably by their doctrines) were to be eschewed (1 Co 1:19 ff).

A near parallel to the New Testament practice in our day can be found in the Pentecostal movement in Sweden. There are no Pentecostal denominations, only local churches in fellowship, each with its own place name.

3.4   HOW BIG SHOULD A LOCAL CHURCH BE?

The New Testament does not give us enough information on this question to enable us to be dogmatic about the size of churches in those times. But some suggestions can be made -

a. *The number of spiritual gifts and/or ministry gifts present*

It appears that local churches were large enough to accommodate a variety of ministries: see 1 Co 12:27 ff; 14:26 ff; Ep 4:11 ff; 1 Ti 3:1 ff; Ph 1:1; Ac 13:1 ff; etc.

On the basis of today's congregations (which may not necessarily be a good guide) this would suggest assemblies of some hundreds of people (for example, Antioch had several prophets and teachers; a church with such multiple leadership today would be hundreds strong).

b. *The number of "founding members"*

In *Jerusalem* (Ac 2:41; 4:5; 6:7), *Samaria* (Ac 8:6, 8, 12), *Derbe* (Ac 14:21), *Ephesus* (Ac 19:17-20), and in other places, large numbers of people (thousands in some cases) came to Christ and formed the nucleus of the churches in those places. Those churches must all have had large congregations.

According to Eusebius, by about AD 250 there were in Rome 46 presbyters, 7 deacons, 7 sub-deacons, 42 acolytes, 52 exorcists, readers, and doorkeepers, and more than 1500 widows and distressed persons. [14] That seems to indicate at least 30,000 Christians! Yet Eusebius refers to this as but *"one church,"* under one bishop (however, he gives no indication as to how many separate meeting places that church may have used).

Then there are other references to churches gathering in a single home - Ro 16:5; 1 Co 16:19; Cl 4:15; Phm 2. And some 350 years later Augustine was still able to write a letter to his friend Juliana, *"be mindful to set me also in your prayers with all your 'household church'"* (op. cit).

It is evident that some churches were very big, while others remained quite small.

c. *The meeting places*

Evangelism was done in many different places: in the temple (Ac 2:1 ff); in *synagogues* (Ac 9:20; 13:5, 14. etc.); in *private homes* (Ac 10:25 ff); in the *open air* (Ac 14:8 ff; 16:13); in *prison* (Ac 16:22 ff); in the *market place* (Ac 17:17 ff); in *debating centers* and *lecture halls* (Ac 17:19 ff; 19:9); and so on.

But regular assemblies seem to have been held in buildings, and often in homes (see references above). The entertaining room in a moderately well-to-do household in the Roman empire could accommodate a maximum of about fifty people. This, of course, poses a question. If congregations were as large as some of those suggested above, how could they possibly meet in such houses?

---

[14] *Ecclesiastical History*, VI 43.

One suggestion is that people regularly met in small groups, only occasionally coming together as *"a whole church"* (cp. Ro 16:5, which may be a reference to one of several *"house churches"* in Rome). 1 Co 11:18 could be read in this way. One writer suggests that the reference to Gaius being hospitable to the whole church (in Corinth?) actually refers to his house being big enough to hold combined meetings there (Ro 16:23).

It is noteworthy that the letter to the Romans is not addressed to a church, but *"to all in Rome"* (1:7). Does this suggest that they did not, in fact, all meet together, but that there were separate meetings (that is, churches)? [15]

4. NEW TESTAMENT ANALOGIES OF THE CHURCH

There are several vivid analogies used in the New Testament to describe the local church. Each sheds some light on the role and mission of the church.

4.1 A BODY

Probably the most significant analogy is that of the human body. Although this analogy is used of the universal church in Ep 1:23, it normally describes the local church. See Ro 12:5; 1 Co 12:12 ff, Ep 4:4, 12, 16.

The idea is most fully developed in 1 Co 12:12 ff. Verse 27 is the key verse. Here Paul makes two basic points:

a. *The local church is Christ's body*

Note that he does not call the Corinthian church a *"part"* of the body of Christ. It *is* Christ's body.

The point is, that each local church cannot be seen as either a hand, or a foot, or a mouth of the larger body of Christ, which together make up the whole body. On the contrary, each local church is the universal church in miniature. Each church is *"a whole body."*

---

[15] Large Pentecostal churches in Sweden and in South America are often set up like this - with one congregation meeting in several places at once.

Indeed, there may be much to commend this concept. Howard Snyder, for instance, argues very powerfully that modern church buildings, used only a few hours a week, are a sinful waste of resources and that such money should be redirected towards the poor and needy. Congregations could then meet as small house groups, combining periodically for large gatherings, which could be in one building owned by all, or in hired premises. (*The Problem of Wineskins,* Inter-Varsity Press, 1977.)

And that in fact is what Paul wrote.

The verse reads literally: "*You are a body of Christ, and members in part.*" Not that there are many "*bodies*" of Christ. Rather, Paul was using a peculiarity of the Greek language to stress the idea that all that belonged to the body of Christ was contained within the local church at Corinth. He did this by omitting the definite article - that is, by writing "*a body of Christ*," and not "*the body of Christ.*" The omission of the definite article has the force of "*stressing the quality of the noun ... just what Christ's body is as to nature and quality, that is what you Corinthians are.*" (Lenski).

This is obviously a major thrust of what Paul is saying. Just as a human body functions as a harmonious whole, so it must be in the body of Christ. Every member must work in harmony with every other so that the body functions as it is intended - vs. 12-26 make this very clear.

*   **Think Spot**: *Paul seems to really labor this point in 1 Co 12. Why? (1 Co 1:10, ff. may give you an idea.)*

How much would he need to labor it if he were writing to the average local church today?

    b. *The charismata enable the local church to function as Christ's body.*

Consider the word "*body.*" What does it mean literally (e.g. as in Luke 24:23)?

This means that the local church is to be the equivalent of Christ's physical presence in the community. What he was among the people in ancient Palestine, the local church is to be among the people today. His ministry is to be carried on by the church. The people should find in the church what they would have found if they had gone to Jesus as he taught and healed on the shores of Galilee.

That is a stunning concept!

*   **Think Spot**: *What were the outstanding features of Jesus' ministry when he was on earth?*

What should be the outstanding features of the local church in its day-by-day ministry?

So Paul points out that God has appointed in the church apostles, prophets, teachers, healers, administrators, etc., to make such a ministry possible. This is why it is essential for a church to recognize apostolic and prophetic gifts - otherwise it can never function as Christ's body!

We can further expand this thought as follows:

- *the authority of Jesus* (Mt 7:28-29) is exercised through the ascension gift ministries: apostles, prophets, evangelists, pastors and teachers (Ep 4:11). This corresponds to the *Head* of Jesus speaking with a voice of authority by the word of God.

- *the power of Jesus* (Mt 8:27, etc.) is exercised through the gifts of the Spirit: word of wisdom, word of knowledge, faith, gifts of healing, working miracles, prophecy, distinguishing of spirits, tongues and interpretation of tongues (1 Co 12:8-11). This corresponds to the *Hands* of Jesus reaching out to help the needy.

- *the grace of Jesus* (2 Co 8:9) is exercised through the fruit of the Spirit: love, joy, peace, patience, kindness, goodness, faithfulness, gentleness and self-control (Ga 5:22-23). This corresponds to the *Heart* of Jesus reaching out in compassion and love.

This analogy of the local church as the body of Christ is exciting and powerful. A similar revelation of the authority of the church is given in Ep 1:18-23.

LESSON TWO

PICTURES OF THE CHURCH

Following on from your last lesson, here are some more colorful ways of looking at the church -

4.2   A TEMPLE

Another analogy is that of the church as a *temple*. Here the points are similar -

a. *Jesus is the cornerstone*

Jesus Christ is the church's bedrock (1 Co 3:11). More specifically, he is the chief cornerstone (Ep 2:20; 1 Pe 2:4, 7-8). There is no other cornerstone for the church.

b. *The prophets and apostles are the foundations*

See Ep 2:20. This possibly refers to the Old Testament and the New Testament - suggesting that faith in Christ and faith in all the scriptures are foundational and fundamental.

c. *Believers are the bricks*

Believers are *"built"* on the foundation and into a holy building by Christ himself (Ep 2:21-22; 1 Pe 2:4-5).

---

*   **Think Spot**: *What are the implications of the phrase "being built together" (Ep 2:22)? Compare the main point of 1 Co 12:12-26.*

---

d. *The temple is to be filled with God's Spirit*

So Peter refers to a *"spiritual house"* (1 Pe 2:5). Paul calls the *"holy temple"* of the church as *"a dwelling in which God lives by his Spirit"* (Ep 2:21-22). Then he spells it out very clearly when he says: *"You ... are God's temple,"* and *"God's Spirit lives in you"* (1 Co 3:16-17 - note that the Greek word used here for *"you"* is plural).

> * **Think Spot**: *How true would it be to say that a congregation where the people are not Spirit filled is like a temple without a god?*

Jesus said he would build his church (Mt 16:18). He is, therefore, both foundation and builder! But this gives us great assurance - a true church is never the work of man but always of Christ!

> * **Think Spot**: *How can we relate this point to Paul's description of himself as "an expert builder" (1 Co 3:10). Does this mean that he, not Christ, is building the church? If not, what does it mean?*

4.3   A HOUSEHOLD

The local church is frequently likened to a household or family (see Ga 6:10; Ep 2:19; 1 Ti 3:15).

This is a simple analogy with obvious implications.

Basically, all the major features of family life apply to local church life. [16] Some of these are -

> *clearly defined membership*
>
> *family privileges*
>
> *family responsibilities*
>
> *family discipline*
>
> *orderliness*
>
> *shared resources*
>
> *leadership.*

> * **Think Spot**: *Can you think of others? Ponder the first point (membership) in the light of the fact that some churches today speak only of "fellowship," not membership.*

---

[16] The church as a family will be more fully discussed later.

4.4   A LAMPSTAND

When John saw his magnificent vision of the risen Christ, he was shown the seven churches of Asia as seven golden lampstands (Re 1:12-20).

There are several points here:

- the local church should be a light to the world (Mt 5:14-16; Ph 2:15);

- as a lampstand needs to be filled with oil, so the church needs to be filled with the Spirit (cp. 1 Co 3:16-17);

- each lampstand is separate, not, as is often thought, a branch of a larger one; that is, each church has its own direct relationship with the risen Christ. Again, we see local churches (rather than "*denominational*" or even "*geographical*" groupings) having this direct relationship with the Lord.

---

*   **Think Spot**: *People sometimes ask, "what is God saying to the church today?" If each church is separately answerable to the risen Christ, is this a valid question? Why, or why not? (Consider what Jesus said to each of the churches in Revelation chapters 2 and 3.)*

4.5   A FIELD

- or, perhaps better, a *Garden.*

Jesus told many parables in which he compared the Kingdom of God to a field or a garden (e.g. Mt 13:1 ff; 13:4 ff; Mk 4:26-34 etc.).

Similarly, Paul compares the church to a harvest field (1 Co 3:9).

Again, there are many obvious parallels -

> *plowing the soil*
>
> *sowing the seed*
>
> *cultivating the seed*
>
> *fertilizing the soil*
>
> *protection from birds of prey*

pruning, etc., as needed

harvesting the crop.

---

*   **Think Spot**: *Can you add to these? Make a list of the spiritual parallels of each, together with scripture references as applicable: for example, plowing the soil = preparation for preaching the gospel (Hosea 10:12).*

Note further that Jesus spoke of both wheat and weeds growing together - i.e. that the church will not be perfect until the day of his coming (Mt 13:30).

He also told us to pray, not for better machinery or equipment or for stronger fences to keep out thieves, but for harvesters to bring in the crop (Mt 9:36-38). Is there a lesson here?

---

*   **Think Spot**: *Are the harvesters of Mt 9:38 and Mt 13:30 the same? If not, how do they differ?*

4.6   A VINE

Similar to the analogy of the church as a field is that of the church as a vine (Jn 15:1 ff).

Here are some of the lessons we can learn -

a. *There is no life apart from Christ (vs. 4-6)*

Just as a branch is lifeless and fruitless when cut off from the vine, so are we when cut off from Christ. Apart from him, how much can we do?

---

*   **Think Spot**: *Of course, apart from him we can in fact do many things. So what does Jesus really mean by "nothing" (vs. 5)?*

---

b. *Discipline and "pruning" are essential for growth (vs. 2)*

Christ can only perfect us when he is able to shape and trim our lives.

> * **Think Spot**: *How does he do this? (Consider Pr 27:17; He 12:4-13.)*

c. *There is the possibility of being "lost" (vs. 6)*

Just as fruitless branches are removed and burned, so Jesus says that any believer who *"does not remain"* in him will be similarly lost.

Note that he does not cut off the offending branch - it removes itself (cp. Jn 10:28-29).

> * **Think Spot**: *Does this mean that one can "lose one's salvation?"*

d. *Fruitfulness is the will of God (vs. 8)*

The aim of growing a vine is to gather a harvest; so the Father is glorified when we bear fruit.

The kind of fruit that glorifies the Father is that which shows us to be Jesus' disciples (vs. 8).

> * **Think Spot**: *What kind of fruit do you think the Lord is talking about here? (Is John 13:35 relevant? See also Ga 5:22-23, and the rest of John 15).*
>
> *Can such "fruit" be fully and effectively produced apart from the local church?*

e. *Answered prayer is related to union with Christ (vs. 7)*

As there can be no fruit on a branch that has been cut off from the vine, so prayers cannot be effectively answered if we are cut off from Christ.

We must remain in union with him, and his words must remain in us. Note that the word *"you"* here is plural - i.e. Jesus is talking to us collectively, not individually.

The importance of the preaching of God's word in a local church is thus clearly seen.

4.7   A BRIDE

This is one of the basic and most beautiful analogies of the church. The *Song of Solomon* is an Old Testament example that has blessed believers for generations. Although the Song is actually a series of love poems between a bridegroom and his bride, it is also an allegorical presentation of the relationship between Christ and the church.

---

*   **Think Spot**: *Read Ca 2:1-7 thinking of yourself as the bride and Christ as the bridegroom.*

Paul makes the classic statement of the church as a Bride in Ep 5:22 ff.

There are three major points -

   a. *The church submits to Christ (vs. 22-24).*

Christ is her head and she is to obey him in everything.

---

*   **Think Spot**: *Does this describe the church you belong to? In what ways could things be improved?*

---

   b. *Christ loved the church (vs. 25 ff).*

First, his love was totally selfless (vs. 25). He gave his life for the church.

Second, this was to make her holy and clean (vs. 28). Like a pure, virgin bride, the church is to be undefiled, without spot or blemish of any kind. It is such a church that will be with the heavenly bridegroom at the great marriage supper of the Lamb (Re 19:6-9).

It is clear that this cleansing of the Bride is Christ's gift (Re 19:8; Ep 5:26-27), made possible through his cross and fully realized at his coming.

---

*   **Think Spot**: *Some people teach that a day is coming when Christians who are ready will be supernaturally cleansed. That is, the Holy Spirit will completely rid them of imperfection, and they will be brought into a condition of...*

> *...full holiness. They, and they alone, will then become the perfect church that Christ will receive as his bride when he returns. Passages such as Ro 8:19; He 9:28 KJV, are also used as evidence.*
>
> *What do you think of that idea?*
>
> *It is surely closer to scripture to teach that the church Christ loves, the church he gave himself for, the church he will cleanse and unite to himself when he appears, is the same church - that is, the whole church of all time, not just that part of it that happens to be alive on earth at the end of this age.*

c. *Christ nourishes and cares for the church (vs. 29).*

Just as a husband must provide basic needs for his wife (cp. Ex 21:11), so Christ cares for his church.

> * **Think Spot**: *If this is so, how can the church ever lack the things it really needs to serve the Lord effectively?*

It is interesting to note that in the parable of the wise and foolish virgins the church is not the Bride (Mt 25:1-13). This parable does not use the bridal analogy, and any attempt to make it do so will result in confused doctrine. The main point of the parable is simply the need to be ready for the bridegroom. It is unnecessary to find some place for the "*bride*" in the interpretation of the parable. Just as Jesus left her out of his story, so can she be left out of the interpretation.

Similarly, some people try to draw a distinction between the church as a "*body*" and the church as a "*bride*." It is suggested that they are different groups, and in fact that the "*bride*" is taken out of the "*body*" - that is, that the "*bride*" is a select company of Christians drawn out of the wider church. That teaching defies both scripture and logic.

4.8   A FLOCK

Another beautiful and simple analogy is that of a flock. This image is common to both Old and New Testaments, and it clearly points out the weaknesses of our humanity and our need of a Shepherd. Hence Isaiah says that *"like sheep"* we have all gone astray (Is 53:6); and Jeremiah laments the false shepherds who scattered the sheep (Je 23:1-2).

However, Jeremiah goes on to promise that the Lord himself will shepherd his people (23:3-6) - a promise that Jesus said was fulfilled in him (Jn 10:1 ff). So he has become the Good Shepherd who really cares for his sheep and gathers them into one flock.

At the human level there are also under-shepherds who care for each local flock and who are themselves answerable to the Chief Shepherd (1 Pe 5:1 ff). [17]

4.9   An Army

See Ep 6:10 ff; 2 Ti 2:1 ff; 1 Ti 6:12.

The *"warfare"* analogy is more an individual emphasis than a collective one; it describes each Christian's conflict with the powers of darkness more than the situation facing the church.

Nonetheless, the church is involved in battle, and it is valid to apply the image of warfare to it. Many Old Testament stories about Israel's struggles against her enemies provide a picture of the reasons for both the victories and the defeats experienced by the church.

Emphasis on the *"warfare"* analogy does create a potential internal peril for the church: the peril of authoritativeness. If the church develops too much of a battle mentality then it will tend toward a military command structure; too much authority will be given to the leaders; a wrongful level of restraint will be placed upon the spiritual liberty under God of each believer. Churches with a strong battle mentality also tend to become aggressive toward the world, to find themselves fighting with man-centered strategies, instead of warring against Satan alone with the weapons of the Spirit (2 Co 10:3-5).

Never forget that the New Testament does not concentrate on the war, but on the victory. We ought not to be groaning because of the conflict but rejoicing because of the triumph!

The Greek verb *"I conquer"* (nikao) is used in the New Testament 28 times, and the noun *"victory"* (*nikos*) 4 times. For examples see Jn 16:33; 1 Jn 2:13-14; 4:4; 5:4-5; Re 2:7, 11, 17, 26; 3:5,12, 21; 12:11; 21:7; 1 Co 15:54, 55, 57; Mt 16:18.

---

[17] See next chapter, section 5, *"The Ministry of Pastor."*

LESSON THREE

APOSTLES AND PROPHETS

It is valuable at times to draw a distinction between *descriptive* and *prescriptive* passages of scripture. The latter are absolute - clear instructions about what we should do or believe. The former are relative - a description of what was done in New Testament days, but not necessarily what *ought* to be done. An obvious example would be

- the apostles evangelized the heathen (prescriptive)

- they used a sailing boat to get there (descriptive)

Much of what we know about New Testament church ministry and structure is descriptive. We know what they did, but we don't know if that is exactly what we should do. In fact, we don't even always know fully what was done.

Gene Getz argues that we need to look at modern church strategy through three *"lenses"* - the lens of scripture, the lens of culture, and the lens of history.

In other words, we must certainly know what the Bible *says*, but we must also be familiar with the lessons of *history*, and aware of the needs of our *culture*. Unless these three *"lenses"* are kept in proper alignment and focus we will have only a fuzzy view of the kind of strategy the church in our day should adopt.

Indeed, it could be argued that the New Testament is deliberately vague in its treatment of church structure and function so that we are free to adopt an approach best suited to the needs of each new generation!

---

*   **Think Spot**: *Can you think of examples of church structures that are outmoded or irrelevant to today's needs. In what way?*

We may even go further and argue that we are not only free to adopt the structure and approach best suited to today's needs, but that we are *obliged* to do so! We need to have sufficient courage to pull down old ways and to pioneer radical new ones, if necessary. This may mean dismantling or selling buildings, changing personnel, surrendering position, accepting a new role, creating new structures; and so on. Few people have the courage to close down or change a well-established institution - but that is sometimes what needs to be done.

> *   **Think Spot**: *Why are people reluctant to face such change? Could you face it? Could you initiate it?*

In what follows, we shall endeavor to look through the *"lens"* of scripture, with some reference to culture and history, so that we can learn, as far as we can, not only what was done in New Testament days, but what is best for us today as well.

Let us begin by looking at the kind of ministry that functioned in the New Testament church, and how it promoted growth and expansion. We shall also see how the same kind of ministry functions today.

The words *"ministry"* and *"minister"* are translations of the Greek words for *"service"* and *"servant"* (i.e. *diakonia* and *diakonos*). That is what the word means in passages like 2 Co 11:15, 23; Ep 3:7; Cl 1:7; 4:7; etc. But because the *"servant"* of each church usually became its leader, the word *"minister"* has now come to mean almost the opposite of what it used to mean!

Both elements will be present in our discussion - namely, leadership and service, for that is what true ministry is all about.

1.   ASCENSION-GIFT MINISTRIES

The major ministry gifts are described and explained in Ep 4:7 ff. They are especially related to Christ's ascension. When he ascended, Christ gave gifts to the church: apostles, prophets, evangelists, pastors and teachers (vs. 11). Concerning these five ministry gifts, note the following -

1.1 THEY WERE GIVEN *AFTER* THE ASCENSION

That is, they apply to the post-ascension church (hence, they are often called "*ascension gifts*"). It cannot then be argued that these ministry gifts were only for New Testament days.

1.2 THE PERSONS THEMSELVES ARE CHRIST'S GIFTS TO THE CHURCH

That is, Paul does not teach that the gift of being an apostle or a prophet is given to certain people, but that the apostles, prophets, etc., are *themselves* gifts to the church. Contrast the gifts of 1 Co 12:8-11; etc.

1.3 THEY REPRESENT THE VICTORY OF THE RISEN CHRIST

Ephesians 4:8 is actually a quotation from Psalm 68:18, which describes the spoil taken in battle by a warrior king. This spoil is then used by him to administer his dominions. (Note the interesting difference between Ps 68:18 and Ep 4:8.)

So Christ, having won the battle over sin, Satan and death, and having taken them captive, as it were, has now ascended and is dispensing gifts by which he administers his kingdom on earth. Clearly, these gifts are to operate with authority from a base of victory, not from struggle and defeat.

1.4 THEY ARE GIVEN TO EQUIP THE SAINTS

The purpose of the five ministry gifts is to prepare God's people for several things (vs. 12-13). These are -

> to serve (i.e. do the work of ministry)
>
> to build up the body of Christ
>
> to bring unity
>
> to know the Son of God
>
> to become mature (lit. "*finished, perfect*")
>
> to measure up to Christ's fullness.

It is self-evident that the need for such gifts is as urgent and desperate today as ever it was.

1.5 THEY ARE GIVEN TO SOLVE CERTAIN PROBLEMS (vs. 14)

These problems are -

> immaturity ("*no longer infants*")
>
> ignorance ("*tossed back and forth*")
>
> deception ("*deceitful scheming*")

Again, since these problems still exist, so does the need for the gifts to overcome them.

1.6 THEY ARE GIVEN TO PROMOTE GROWTH AND LOVE (vs. 15-16)

Only when these two factors are evident can the church effectively fulfill its task. Hence, we may also refer to these gifts as "*growth gifts*" - for that is their aim.

Furthermore, this gives us a valid test for such gifts - where there is no spiritual growth, there may be no genuine gift.

1.7 THE FOLLOWING DIAGRAM ILLUSTRATES THE MEANING OF EP 4:11-15

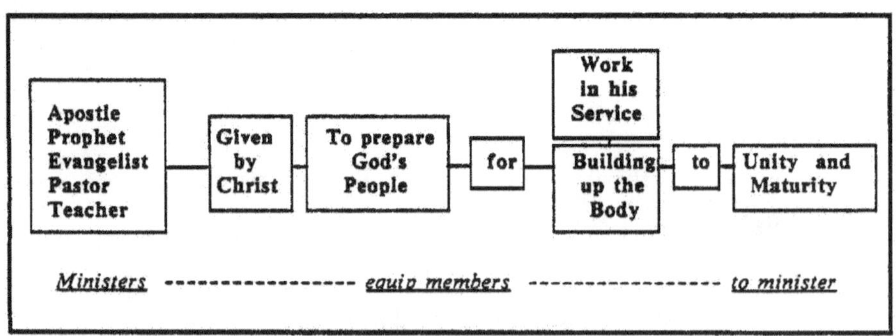

2. THE MINISTRY OF AN APOSTLE

The first, and most would say, the chief of the ascension-gift ministries is that of an apostle. The Greek word is *apostolos* = a person who is sent with authority; a special messenger; an emissary or envoy. It is used 81 times in the New Testament. A related verb is *apostellein* - to send forth.

In New Testament terms, an apostle is a special messenger of Christ, but also much more than that.

2.1   PAUL IS THE PREEMINENT MODEL OF APOSTOLIC MINISTRY

a. He was commissioned supernaturally by the ascended Christ (Ac 9:1 ff; 26:15-18; 1 Co 9:1; Ga 1:11 ff; Ep 1:1; 1 Ti 1:1; etc.). Clearly, an apostle must have a sense of divine mission and calling.

b. He founded churches, and established them in an orderly fashion and in sound doctrine and practice (Ac 13:1-14, 28; 15:36; 18:22-23; 21:17; etc.). Such churches were in fact *"proof"* of his ministry (1 Co 9:1-3). An apostle is thus a pioneer, able to open up new areas to the kingdom of God.

c. He was sent out by a local church. See Ac 13:1 ff. This was normally reckoned to be an essential credential (cp. Ac 18:27; 28:21; 2 Co 8:16 ff); but Paul did not hesitate to point to the fruit of his ministry as being an adequate credential by itself (cp. 2 Co 3:1 ff.)

d. He exercised supernatural gifts (Ac 14:8 ff). 19:11; Ro 15:18-19; He 2:3-4). Paul calls signs, wonders, and miracles the *"things that mark an apostle"* (2 Co 12:12, NIV). Apostolic ministry is, therefore, a supernatural ministry.

e. He taught the churches he founded. This is self-evident by the letters he wrote. Teaching is an essential ingredient of the ministry of an apostle.

f. He exercised authority and care over the churches he founded (2 Co 11:28). This also is self- evident by the letters he wrote. Thus -

> - he commended them (1 Co. 11:2)
>
> - he rebuked them (1 Co 11:17; Ga 1:6 ff)
>
> - he instructed them in specific areas of conduct, etc. (1 Co 5:5; 16:1; 2 Th 3:6-15)
>
> - he expected them to obey his commands (2 Co 12:14 ff; Ph 2:12; 2 Th 3:12-14).

An apostle has authority and ministry beyond and above that of local churches together.

g. He also taught and exercised authority over churches that he did not himself found (e.g. Rome and Colosse). Although he does not openly rebuke those two churches, he still gives them specific instructions (e.g. Cl 4:1 ff). Apostolic ministry may be recognized beyond churches directly founded by the apostle.

> * **Think Spot**: *What limitations or restraints are there on such authority? Consider*
>
> *-the sovereignty of the local churches*
>
> *-the implications of refusal to accept such authority (What if his authority is refused? What can the apostle do?)*

h. He exercised all of the growth-gifts at different times. That is, the ministry-functions of a

> - prophet (Ac 13:1; 1 Co 14:6; Ro 11:25 ff; Ac 20:22 ff; 27:22 ff). He also exhorted, edified and consoled (cp. 1 Co 14:3, and the content of Paul's letters).
>
> - evangelist (1 Co 9:16-18).
>
> - pastor (2 Co 11:28; Ac 15:36; 20:17-37). See above on his care of the churches
>
> - teacher. See all of his letters.

Thus, apostolic ministry really embraces all of the growth-gifts and is a combination of them all. (Of course, Paul is the outstanding model of an apostle - few other apostles may reach his heights. But any apostolic ministry will follow this pattern in some degree.)

2.2   Is Apostolic Ministry Extant Today?

It is commonly believed

- that there were only 12 apostles;

- or that apostles existed in New Testament times only;

- or that apostles are not needed today.

But you should note the following -

a. The 12 apostles have a special place in the kingdom. They were foundational to the New Testament church (Ep 2:20) and their names are recorded in the new Jerusalem (Re 21:14). However, the fact that Matthias replaced Judas and was not one of the original 12, suggests that the number 12 is symbolic rather than literal, and that others may still be added to that original band of men.

        b. The ministry-gift of "apostle" was given after the ascension of Christ. Therefore, these post-ascension apostles must necessarily exclude the 12.

        c. There is considerable New Testament evidence of apostles other than the original 12. Consider the following:

Paul (Ac 14:4,14; Ro 1:1; 11:13; 1 Co 1:1; etc.)

Barnabas (Ac 14:4, 14)

James (1 Co 15:7; Ga 1:19)

Silas (Ac 15:40; 16:19 ff; 17:4 ff; 1 Th 1:1; and 2:7)

Silvanus (= Silas? 2 Co 1:19; 1 Th 1:1; 2 Th 1:1)

Andronicus (Ro 16:7)

Junia (Ro 16:7)

Titus and *"two brothers"* (2 Co 8:16-24)

Timothy (by implication, 2 Co 1:19; Ph 2:19-24; 1 Th 1:2 and 2:7; 1, 2 Ti)

Apollos (by implication - 1 Co 1:12; 3:4-5, 22; 16:12

Clement (Ph 4:2)

Euodia (Ph 4:2)

Syntyche (Ph 4:3)

2.3   To What Extent Did an Apostle Exercise Authority Over Local Churches?

As we have seen in the case of Paul, an apostle can speak with authority to local churches, especially those which he himself has founded. This is self-evident from Paul's letters (see above 2.1, e and f). So Paul freely exercised the right to move people around in ministry (for example, Tit 1:5; 3:12-14; 1 Ti 1:3 ff), although, where possible, he obviously did this in consultation with the churches concerned (2 Co 8:16 ff, especially vs. 19).

(The relationship between ministry gifts and churches will be discussed further in a later section.)

2.4   TO WHAT EXTENT IS AN APOSTLE SUBJECT TO HIS OWN LOCAL CHURCH?

Paul and Barnabas were originally commissioned by their church at Antioch (Ac 13:1-3). At the end of their journey, they returned to Antioch, where they stayed *"a long time"* (Ac 14:28). They had been gone at least a year, possibly two (authorities differ in their calculations).

Paul decided by himself to make the second journey and chose Silas as his companion, but was then "commended by the brothers" (Ac 15:36-41). This time, he returned first to Jerusalem (*"the church"*), and then to Antioch where he spent *"some time"* (Ac 18:22-23). But before then they had stayed at least one and a half years in Corinth (Ac 18:11), and were away possibly three years altogether.

Paul's third journey also involved between two and three years, mostly at Ephesus (Ac 19:10; 20:31), and possibly took four years altogether. After this, Paul and his companions returned to Jerusalem.

Clearly, Paul regarded Antioch as his base, and he also saw the need to relate to the original apostles in Jerusalem. None of the early church leaders believed that they could effectively serve God in isolation from their peers or from the influence of the local churches. Hence there are many indications in the New Testament of the manner in which the apostles worked together: Ac 13:2; 15:37, 40; 17:14-15; 1 Th 1:1; Ga 2:1-9; Ph 1:1; Cl 1:1; Ro 16:1 ff; Ac 19:22; 20:1-6.

It is equally clear however, that when Paul was away from Antioch, the church there had little influence over him. Likewise, at no time did he allow any other apostle more than a limited authority over him. He was prepared to accept the right of the apostles to assess his ministry, but in the end he insisted on his own right to be answerable to God alone. See Ga 2:6-14.

The 2nd century document, *The Didache* (c. AD 150), makes this interesting comment on apostles -

> *"Every apostle who comes to you should be welcomed as the Lord, but he is not to stay more than a day, or two days if it is really necessary. If he stays for three days, he is no genuine apostle. If he asks for money, he is not a genuine apostle ..."* (2:11).

This seems to provide a balance to the authority of the apostle - he has only as much authority as the congregation is willing to give him. His authority is spiritual, not institutional. That is, it is the authority of the ministry, not the authority of the man that is important.

2.5   CAN A WOMAN BE AN APOSTLE?

Rengstorf argues that:

- there is no New Testament record of a woman apostle.

- the Hebrew equivalent of *apostolos* is a legal term, and women had "very restricted legal competence" in Judaism.

- there is no feminine form of the word *apostolos* used in the New Testament (see Kittel, 1 p. 421).

On the other hand, it may be pointed out that

-there is no feminine form of the word *diakonos* (deacon, minister), but the masculine is used for Phoebe, a woman, in Ro 16:1 (that is, the Greek word is "deacon," not "deaconess," as in the RSV).

- the name "Junia" (Ro 16:7) is actually a woman's name, although changed to the masculine "Junias" by most (male?) translators. Is this evidence of a woman apostle?

What was the ministry of Priscilla and Aquila, both of whom were called by Paul his *"fellow workers?"* (Ro 16:3; and see also Ac 18:2, 18, 26; 1 Co 16:19). And what about Euodia and Syntyche? (Ph 4:2-3). In the cases of both Junia and Priscilla, it would seem that they shared ministry with their husbands (assuming that Andronicus was the husband of Junia). Otherwise, many commentators would argue, 1 Ti 2:11 ff would seem to rule out any apostolic ministry for a woman.

The word "missionary" (Latin. *mitto* - I send) is based on the same idea as the word "apostle." Is there any objection to women missionaries? As William Booth once said: "Some of the best men are women!"

Other commentators allow that women may be called to serve the church as preachers, teachers, "special messengers" (*apostolos*), and the like; but that 1 Ti 2:11 ff prevents them from holding the senior pastor's office in a local church. Others argue that Paul prohibits women from holding any senior preaching or pastoral role in the church. But that is a debate we cannot enter into here.

3. THE MINISTRY OF A PROPHET

The Greek word is *prophetes* = one who proclaims; one who speaks forth; possibly also one who foretells. It is used 149 times in the New Testament (see Kittel, 6, 784 ff).

The ministry of prophet is widely recognized in scripture, although little understood today.

3.1 PROPHETS IN THE OLD TESTAMENT

Old Testament prophets were known by several names

- prophet (from *nabi* = "proclaimer;" 1 Sa 10:5 ff; De 18:1 ff; Am 3:7-8).

- prophet (from *chozeh*, of uncertain derivation; 2 Sa 24:11; Am 7:12).

- man of God (e.g. 1 Sa 9:6 ff; De 33:1; etc.)

- servant of God (2 Kg 17:13, 23; Je 7:25; etc.)

- seer (1 Sa 9:9; 2 Kg 17:13; 1 Ch 29:29; etc.)

All of these terms can also be applied, of course, to New Testament prophets.

3.2 AMOS IS A SUITABLE MODEL OF THE OLD TESTAMENT PROPHET

- he was not a professional prophet (7:14)

- he spoke the word of the Lord (7:15-17)

- he was called to prophesy (7:14-15)

- he showed social concern (ch. 2, 6, 8)

- he was a seer with prophetic vision and insight (ch. 7-9)

- he was a poet (ch. 1-2, 4-5; etc.)

- he had a zeal for God (3:1-8)

- his message was actually unheeded

- he spoke of impending judgment (6:8-14)

- he spoke of future blessing (9:13-15)

Many of those elements may be in New Testament prophecy (for the marks of a false prophet, see Jeremiah ch. 23).

3.3 PROPHETS IN THE NEW TESTAMENT

Prophets are included in all New Testament lists of charismatic gifts (1 Co 12:8-11, 28-31; Ro 12:3-8; Ep 4:11). There are also several specific examples

- Agabus and others (Ac 11:26-30; 21:10-14)

- Judas and Silas (Ac 15:32)

- Barnabas and others at Antioch (Ac 13:1-3)

- Corinthian prophets (1 Co 14:29-30)

- Philip's daughters (Ac 21:9)

- various New Testament writers (e.g. Jude)

Note: while all believers may prophesy (1 Co 14:31, 39), not all are prophets (12:39), just as all believers may evangelize or teach without being designated evangelists or teachers. The distinction, therefore, between a prophet and other Christians is one of degree more than one of kind. That is, the prophet is a person with an extraordinary prophetic ability. He (or she) is a "prophet," not because he holds a certain office in the church, but because he has a certain ability. The designation "prophet" is not a title of office, but a description of work or function within the church. (As far as the New Testament is concerned, of course, the same is true of an apostle, evangelist, pastor, or teacher.)

3.4 THE NATURE OF NEW TESTAMENT PROPHECY

There are four basic elements to New Testament prophecy. These are:

- revelation (Ac 11:27-30; 13:1-2; 1 Co 14:24-25, 31; Re 1:10-11; 4:1-2; 17:3; 21:10).

- edification (i.e. building up, strengthening - 1 Co 14:3, 5, 17).

- exhortation (i.e. encouragement - 1 Co 14:3, 31; Ac 15:32; Hg 1:3 ff).

- consolation (i.e. comfort - 1 Co 14:3; Ac 15:32).

It is clear that all of these functions are as much in need in the church today as they ever were. (Note that the element of correction or rebuke is much more an element of Old Testament, rather than New Testament, prophecy.)

> *   **Think Spot**: *What about the concept that the charismatic gift of prophecy is redundant now that we possess a complete New Testament?*

It is also clear that a prophet's ministry may be very broad, including inspirational preaching and teaching. Not just foretell, but forth-tell (cp. Ex 7:1).

> *   **Think Spot**: *Are there prophets in the church today who are largely unrecognized? Do you know of any?*

3.5   THE SOURCE OF NEW TESTAMENT PROPHECY

The ministry of the prophet is given to the church by the ascended Christ. It is essentially a supernatural ministry. Yet like all of the ministry gifts, it is consistent with and related to natural abilities.

The gift of prophecy (which a prophet by definition must have) together with the accompanying gifts of word of knowledge and word of wisdom, are gifts of the Spirit (1 Co 12:8-11), and are supernatural in character. Is this one reason why the more "natural" gifts of pastor and teacher have survived, while those of prophet and apostle have become rare?

3.6   THE EXERCISE OF PROPHETIC MINISTRY

Prophetic ministry may be exercised as the result of several factors.

a. *The sovereignty of God*

As in the case of Caiaphas (Jn 11:51-42), prophets may speak prophetically without even knowing that they are doing so.

b. *Revelation*

On the other hand, a prophet may be well aware that God has revealed something to him and that he must speak it forth. There are many Old Testament examples of this (Je 1:4 ff; 20:9; Ez 1:1 ff; Am 7:11; etc.). In fact, according to Nu 12:6 ff; this is God's normal method. See also 1 Co 14:26, 30; etc.

c. *Faith*

Then again, note that a prophet, knowing that he is a prophet, may see the need to proclaim a prophetic word and so simply speak out by faith, trusting God for it. This seems to be especially emphasized in the New Testament. See Ro 12:3 ff; 1 Co 14:32; 2 Ti 1:6. Indeed, this is the faith principle for the use of all spiritual gifts (e.g. Mt 14:22 ff; 14:29; 2 Kg 4:1-7).

This is why, ultimately, the validity of the gift does not depend on holiness etc. It is dependent upon God by faith. When a prophet speaks by faith, although he may be mistaken about many other matters, he must believe that a prophetic word given by faith will be right (and he will not be afraid to have it tested either!) (This concept is similar to that of the Pope being "infallible" when he speaks ex cathedra.)

Site of the ancient city of Lystra, where a notable miracle occurred (Ac. 14:8-10), and where Paul and Barnabus nearly became part of Greek mythology! (vs.11-18)

---

*   **Think Spot**: *Note that a prophet may not always understand what he is saying (see 2 Pe 1:21). Even more, he may actually speak in riddles (Nu 11:6 ff). What is the benefit of this for the hearer?*

3.7   RESTRICTIONS ON PROPHETIC MINISTRY

a. *Believer-priesthood*

In Old Testament days, a prophet was often God's mouthpiece to the nation. Under the New Testament, every believer is a "priest" (1 Pe 2:9; Re 1:6), and therefore has direct access to God (He 10:19-23). Any prophetic utterance needs to be balanced and weighed in the light of one's own convictions. Paul made it plain that he had either the right to reject a prophecy, or at least to determine for himself what influence he would allow the prophecy to have over him (see Ac 20:22 ff). So also, Agabus was heeded on one occasion (Ac 11:27-30), but ignored on another (21:10-14).

b. *Evaluation by the Church*

All prophetic statements must be subject to testing, either by the rest of the church, or by other prophets, or in some other responsible manner (1 Co 14:29; 1 Th 5:20-21). The requirement that prophetic sayings must be evaluated or judged by the church indicates that normally prophets were expected to speak in a public setting, not a private one. The private use of prophecy was certainly uncommon in the New Testament church, if not quite unknown. There are false prophets as well as true (Lu 6:26; Mt 24:24), and the best protection against being led astray is to allow prophesying only within the shelter of the church or under its firm oversight. [18]

The basic tests of all prophecy are two-fold

- is it biblical? (1 Jn 4:1ff; De 13:1-5; Je 23:16 ff; Ne 6:10 ff)

-is it true? (that is, will it come to pass? De 18:21-22).

The mere fact that a prophet has spoken does not mean that the message is infallible, any more than it did in Old Testament days (cp. Ne 6:14; Je 23:25 ff; 28:1-17; cp. De 17:6).

It is interesting that *The Didache* claims that while a prophet is speaking in the Spirit he should "on no account" be subject to any tests. But it goes on to say that not all who speak in the Spirit are prophets, "unless they exhibit the manners and conduct of the Lord." For "it is by their behavior that you can tell the impostor from the true." His "deeds must correspond to his words." So if he calls out for money for himself, he is false. But if in the Spirit he bids the people to give to others, "nobody should criticize him" (2:11)

---

[18] This does not mean that prophesying in a private setting must be forbidden, but only that you should not accept the authority of a prophetic revelation until it has been subject to responsible testing.

Thus, a third test is introduced: is the prophet's manner of life consistent? (Although this is not necessarily determinative; even someone who is not living a consistent life may give a valid prophecy - e.g. Jn 11:51-52)

> *   **Think Spot**: *It is actually essential that this should be so. Why? Also, what bearing does the use of the first person singular ("I say to you my people"), or a phrase like "thus says the Lord" have on the validity of a prophecy? Should such terminology be used?*

3.8   THE POWER OF PROPHECY

While cautions have been expressed about being too ready to accept the words of a prophet, there may be, on the other hand, great power in what he says. So Paul encouraged Timothy to use words spoken about him in prophecy as weapons by which he could *"fight a good fight"* (1 Ti 1:18). Similarly, it was through prophecy that a gift (*charisma*) was imparted to him (1 Ti 4:14. See also Je 1:12).

A prophet's ministry may, therefore, be life-changing.

3.9   THE FUNCTION OF PROPHETS

While prophets were sometimes attached to a local church (Ac 13:1), they were often itinerant; e.g. Judas and Silas (Ac 15:22, 32); Agabus and his fellow-prophets (Ac 11:27 ff; 21:10).

This is confirmed by *The Didache* -

"Everyone who comes 'in the name of the Lord' is to be made welcome, though later on you must test him and find out about him. You will be able to distinguish the true from the false. If the newcomer is only passing through, give him all the help you can - though he is not to stay more than a couple of days with you, or three if it is unavoidable. But if he wants to settle down among you and is a skilled worker, let him find employment and earn his bread. If he knows no trade, use your discretion to make sure that he does not live in idleness simply on the strength of being a Christian ..."

"A genuine prophet, however, who wishes to make his home with you has a right to a livelihood ... You are therefore to take the first products of your winepress, your threshing-floor, your oxen and your sheep, and give them as first-fruits to the prophets, for nowadays it is they who are your 'High Priest' ... Similarly, when you broach a jar of wine or oil, take the first portion to give it to the prophets." [19]

From this passage, several matters of practical interest are raised -

a. *Prophets were often itinerant*. Indeed, this was essential if the whole body of Christ were to benefit.

b. *Prophetic ministry*, like apostolic, was an integrating ministry, promoting unity and strengthening ties between churches.

c. *Local churches* accepted their responsibility to support genuine ministry.

d. *Prophets were not accepted uncritically*. Local churches saw their right to assess and evaluate any itinerant ministry and either to accept it or reject it. Hence, like an apostle, a prophet only had as much authority as people gave him - his also was a spiritual, not an institutional authority.

3.10 CAN A WOMAN BE A PROPHET?

The Old Testament mentions many prophetesses, including

- Miriam (Ex 15:20)

- Deborah (Jg 4:4)

- Huldah (2 Kg 22:14)

- Isaiah's wife (Is 8:3)

In the New Testament, there is reference to Ann (Lu 2:36) and to the false prophetess, Jezebel (Re 2:20).

Philip had four daughters who prophesied (Ac 21:9). It was foretold by Joel that in the New Testament era *"sons and daughters"* would prophesy (Jl 2:28; Ac 2:17-18). Paul speaks of women praying and prophesying (1 Co 11:5).

---

[19] From *Early Christian Writings*, tr. by M. Staniforth; Penguin Books, UK, 1968; "The Didache," sec. 12-13; pg. 233-234. Staniforth actually translates the Greek word in this passage, not as "prophet" but "charismatist."

It seems clear that women, as well as men, may be numbered among the prophets.

3.11 FORMS OF PROPHECY

The forms that prophecies take may well be as varied as the people who prophesy.

Prophetic utterance may be in song (1 Ch 25:1; the Psalms); spoken word (Is, Je, etc.); symbol (Agabus - Ac 21:10-11; or Ezekiel - Ez 4:1 ff; 5:1 ff); parable (Nathan - 2 Sa 12:1 ff); scripture (Paul - Ac 28:25-29); and so on.

God uses people as they are, and the form of their message will be appropriate both for them and the people to whom they speak.

Lesson Four

Evangelists, Pastors and Teachers

We began in your last lesson a study of the five ministry-gifts the ascended Christ has given to the church. We have so far considered apostles and prophets. Now we look at the remaining three ministries -

1. The Ministry of an Evangelist

Etymology:

evangelistes	= a speaker of good news (3 times in N.T.)
from *evangelion*	= good news (76 times in N.T.)
and *evangelidzesthai*	= to bring good news; to bear good tidings (51 times in N.T.)

The noun "good news" and the verb "to bring good news" were both common in secular Greek (e.g. to bring news of victory in battle). The noun "speaker of good news" was rare - as it is in the N.T.

These terms came to have special "Christian" meanings like "*gospel*" (good news), and "*evangelist*" (bearer of good news), etc.

So an evangelist is essentially one who speaks the good news about Jesus Christ.

1.1 Philip is a Useful Model of an Evangelist

Philip is called "*the evangelist*" in Ac 21:8 - making it clear that he had a recognized ministry in this area. If we use him as a model, we find the following features of evangelistic ministry -

a. He was "*full of wisdom*" (Ac 6:3-5)

See Jesus' words in Mt 10:16 and consider their relevance (see also 1 Co 3:10).

b. He was a *"servant"* (Ac 6:1-5)

Philip's first ministry was that of waiting on tables and caring for widows. Those who learn to serve can later be used more widely. (The office of " minister" or "deacon" is basic to all others.)

c. He was *"full of faith"* (Ac 6:5)

I assume that what was true of Stephen was also true of Philip: he was powerful in faith. No doubt this should apply to any ministry, but it certainly applies to that of the evangelist. Because his ministry takes him to new areas, he needs faith to break through the dominion of darkness.

---

*   **Think Spot**: *Consider the significance of the word "full" in the phrase "full of faith." What are its implications?*

---

d. He was *"full of the Holy Spirit"* (Ac 6:3, 5)

Again, while this applies to all ministries, it must be true of the evangelist, who certainly needs to be led by the Spirit, and made successful by the Spirit (see also Lu 24:49; Ac 1:8).

e. His message was *"Christ"* (Ac 8:5)

The fact that Jesus was the Messiah was central to Philip's preaching (see also 8:35).

f. *He worked miracles* (Ac 8:6-7)

The signs and wonders that Philip performed caused the people to listen to his message.

g. *He baptized his converts* (Ac 8:12)

Baptism was seen as their public confession of Christ - Philip encouraged this.

h. *He did not impart the Holy Spirit* (Ac 8:15)

The reason for this is not clear - although many suggestions have been offered. Perhaps as an evangelist he saw his role only as introducing them to Christ.

i. *He was willing to preach anywhere* (Ac 8:26 ff)

He was prepared to leave the admiring crowds of Samaria and go to a lone individual in the desert.

j. *He was led by the Spirit* (Ac 8:26, 29)

Being *"full of the Holy Spirit,"* he could hear the voice of the Spirit.

k. *He used a simple question approach* (Ac 8:30)

That is, he adapted his method to suit each new situation and audience by choosing proclamation, or miracles, or argument, or dialogue, etc.

l. *He preached whenever he got the opportunity* (Ac 8:40)

m. *Unanswered questions*

There are many unanswered questions about Philip's ministry; for example:

- how was he supported?

- did he have a local church "home?" (He did not return to Jerusalem, but settled in Caesarea, Ac 8:40; 21:8, where there was evidently no church, Ac 10:1 ff.)

- did he "report back" to the apostles? (Ac 8:14)

- what did he do with his converts? (The apostles cared for those at Samaria, but what about those referred to in Acts 8:40? Some similar provision was no doubt made.)

The answer to these questions seem to be left open - perhaps for us to work out in the best way in the light of our present circumstances and need.

1.2 WHAT IS THE MESSAGE OF THE EVANGELIST?

It may be summarized in the following scriptures:

Lu 3:18; 4:18

Ac 5:42

Ac 8:1ff

1 Co 15:1-2

Ga 1:8, 11, 16, 23; etc.

It can be seen also in the early preaching of the apostles; for example, see Ac 3:12 ff; 7:1 ff; 10:34 ff.

Essentially, it is a declaration of the simple story of Jesus Christ, with special emphasis on his saving work; that is, on his death, burial and resurrection.

> *   **Think Spot**: *Many "evangelists" today travel from church to church preaching "faith," praying for the sick, etc. Is this really "evangelism?" If not, what is it? (Compare the ministry of a prophet).*

1.3   WHAT IS THE MOTIVATION OF AN EVANGELIST?

For every ministry gift, God gives faith to help it to function (Ro 12:3 ff). For the evangelist, there must also be an inner, yearning compulsion so that he cannot rest unless he preaches the gospel. (See 1 Co 9:150-16; cp. Je 20:9). He is confident that God will bring about a harvest (Mk 4:26-29).

1.4   CAN A WOMAN BE AN EVANGELIST?

Why not?

(Aimee McPherson used to love to point out that the very first preaching of the good news of the resurrection was done by a woman!)

2.   THE MINISTRY OF A PASTOR

Etymology:

poimen   = shepherd (18 times in N.T.)

2.1   WHAT IS A PASTOR?

It is ironic that although the English word "pastor" occurs only once in most English translations of the Bible (Ep 4:11), more ministers are known as "pastor" than anything else!

However, if we take the word in its original meaning of "shepherd," we find that it appears quite frequently ("pastor" is simply the Latin word for "shepherd").

In plain terms, the pastor's task is to act as a shepherd for the people who make up the flock of God.

2.2   JESUS - THE MODEL PASTOR

The ideal model of a pastor is given in the teaching of Jesus himself in Jn 10:1 ff. As the Chief Shepherd or Chief Pastor (1 Pe 5:4) he gives the ultimate example to

all other shepherds (1 Pe 5:2-3). See also Mt 9:36; 25:32; 26:31; Mk 6:34; 14:27; He 13:20; 1 Pe 2:25.

This was in fulfillment of the prophecy of Jeremiah who spoke judgment on the shepherds who scattered and forsook the flock, and then promised good shepherds who would be ruled by *"the Lord our Righteousness"* (Je 23:2- 6).

Concerning the Chief Shepherd, note the following (from Jn 10) -

a. *He has authority* (vs. 1-2)

In biblical times the imagery of a shepherd contained the idea of authority as well as that of nurture. This authority was expressed through the concept of a legitimate sovereignty. So, a lawful king had a duty both to rule and to succor his people, and he could boldly assert his right to the throne. When Jesus called himself "Shepherd" he was claiming that he had a true and lawful authority over the flock of God.

b. *He knows his sheep by name* (vs. 3, 14-15)

He knows each one individually - not just the flock as a whole.

* **Think Spot**: *How can this be done in a large church?*

c. *The sheep listen to his voice* (vs. 3, 27)

He is respected and heeded by the people.

d. *He leads the sheep* (vs. 3-4, 27)

Note how he leads by "going ahead of them" (NIV). He does not "drive" from behind. The shepherd must know where he is going before he can take the sheep there.

e. *The sheep follow him* (vs. 4-5)

A true leader is always followed - but people will turn away from a shepherd who does not lead ("they will run away from him").

f. *He feeds the sheep* (vs. 9)

The people are free "to come in and go out" - but as he provides pasture, so they are fed (contrast Je 23:2-3).

g. *He gives life to the sheep* (vs. 10, 28)

Just as the Chief Shepherd gives abundant life, so each pastor must also give life to his people: that is, they must flourish under his care (cp 2 Co. 3:7-9).

h. *He lays down his life for the sheep* (vs. 11, 15, 17-18)

The spirit of a true pastor is one of total self-giving for the sake of the sheep. The sheep do not exist for him - he exists for them and will die for them if necessary.

i. *He protects the sheep* (vs. 12-13, 28-29)

When the flock is attacked, he is there to uphold and protect it.

j. *He unites the sheep* (vs. 16)

The ideal is for one flock to be united beneath the care of one shepherd. Each flock should be so united.

k. *He enlarges the flock* (vs. 16)

Other sheep must be constantly added to the flock, for two reasons:

- their mutual safety.

- otherwise the flock will die out.

l. *He goes after any stray sheep* (Lu 15:1-7)

The above model cam be supplemented by reference to the actual life and ministry of Jesus. The principles laid down here, however, provide a firm and lasting basis for pastoral ministry. [20]

2.3   PASTORS AND ELDERS

When we note that the word "pastor" means "shepherd," and also that it is the duty of elders to "shepherd" the sheep, it is clear that the terms "pastor" and "elder" are synonymous:

- Peter instructs elders to "be shepherds (*poimaino*) of God's flock" and to look to the "Chief Shepherd" (1 Pe 5:1-4 NIV); that is, to be pastors.

- Paul uses almost identical terms to the Ephesian elders when he says, "Be shepherds (*poimaino*) of the church of God" (Ac 20:28). Again, it means "to be pastors."

---

[20] It is also interesting to note that in the whole of Jn 10:1-18 nothing is said about punishing the sheep if they do wrong.

Similar cross-references between 1 Ti 3:1 ff and Tit 1:6 ff also show that the terms *presbuteros* ("elder") and *episkopos* ("bishop") are synonymous (note especially Tit 1:6-7).

What then is the difference between "elder" and "bishop?" "Elder" was a term more familiar to Jews, and it conveyed the idea of status; but "bishop" was a term familiar to Greeks, and it indicated function. Both ideas are found in the New Testament use of these words, sometimes with a separate emphasis, sometimes combined.

It is probably also valid to assume that *"the gifts of administration"* (or of "government") mentioned in 1 Co 12:28 refer to the same office and function (that is, to the office of elder and function of bishop). The same applies to the references to *"leaders"* in 1 Th 5:12 and He 13:7. See also Mt 2:6, where the terms *"leader"* and *"shepherd"* are both applied to Christ.

Hence the following terms appear to be more or less synonymous - [21]

poimen	= shepherd, pastor
presbuteros	= elder
episkopos	= overseer, bishop
kubernesis	= administrator, governor
hegoumenos	= leader

This suggests, then, that no-one should be appointed an elder unless he could also be appointed as a pastor/leader etc.

2.4 WHAT ARE THE QUALIFICATIONS OF PASTORS?

A composite list may be compiled from the pastoral letters and 1 Peter as follows:

> above reproach
>
> married to one wife
>
> temperate
>
> self-controlled
>
> respectable
>
> hospitable
>
> able to teach

---

[21] A more detailed discussion of this can be found below.

not given to wine

gentle

peaceable

not a lover of money

managing his family well

mature

of good reputation

having obedient children

not overbearing

honest

a lover of good

upright

holy

disciplined

holding firmly to the gospel message

able to present sound doctrine

able to refute error

eager to serve

an example

(1 Ti 3:1 ff; Tit 1:6 ff; 1 Pe 5:1 ff).

It is clear that anyone who seeks the office of pastor must measure up to very stringent standards of personal character and behavior.

In fact, it appears that to Paul, personal qualities were of greater importance than personal abilities.

2.5   WHAT ARE THE DUTIES OF A PASTOR?

In his instructions to Timothy and Titus, Paul describes mainly the personal qualifications of character that a pastor/elder needs. So he says little about what such a man does. Even so, it is possible to list several basic duties -

a. *He teaches the word* (1 Ti 3:2; Tit 1:9; He 13:7)

b. *He is an administrator and overseer* (1 Tit 5:17-18)

Note that this verse suggests that administration and teaching may be separate functions of eldership; that is, a pastor may basically be either one or the other.

c. *He works hard* (1 Th 5:12)

d. *He admonishes and keeps watch over the church* (1 Th 5:12; He 13:17)

e. *He is willing to accept responsibility*

- for he is answerable to God for his task (He 13:17). He thus bears a greater burden than others (Ja 3:1).

f. *He is a good shepherd of the flock* (Ac 20:28; 1 Pe 5:2)

See above on Jesus as the model.

g. *He is an example* (1 Pe 5:3)

h. *He ministers to the sick* (Ja 5:14 ff)

- and must therefore be a man of faith.

i. *He cares for widows and orphans*

- and for others in need, as implied in Paul's letter to Timothy.

j. *He does not abuse his authority*

- by "interfering" or "lording it" over the flock (1 Pe 5:1-4; Ja 5:16; Ph 2:4).

Note: In a fascinating study on celestial eldership in the Book of Revelation, Geoffrey Bingham notes the following features about these elders:

they have authority

they are pure

they are close to the throne (closer even than angels)

they have intimate knowledge of God

they sing a "new song"

they are skilled in worship

they bring prayers of the saints

they speak for God.

See Re 4:2 ff; 5:8 ff; 7:13-17; 11:17-18; 19:1ff; etc. [22]

---

[22] *Living Faith Study*, No. 22.

2.6   SHOULD THERE BE ONLY ONE PASTOR IN A CHURCH?

As noted above, Jesus spoke of "one flock" and "one shepherd" (Jn 10:16). However, an eastern flock usually numbered no more than 500, with many small flocks of 20-50. Can one man handle a spiritual flock of more than this? Or should even a small flock have more than one shepherd?

Beautiful old churches like these are now outdated. More modern structures are favoured for the new worship styles.

       a. *It is desirable for the shepherd to know each sheep individually.*

See above on Jn 10:3, 14-15. A large flock can be divided into smaller flocks so that each "under-shepherd" knows each of his sheep by name (note, however, that to know 1000 or more people by name is by no means impossible).

       b. *The word "elder" often occurs in the plural in the N.T.*

See Ac 14:23; 15:2, 4, 6, 22-23; 16:4; 20:17; 21:18; 1 Ti 5:17; Ja 5:14; 1 Pe 5:1; Ph 1:1. See also He 13:7, 17.

These references are not entirely helpful because of our ignorance of the size and number of congregations in each place mentioned. However, it does appear that a plurality of elders was normal.

        c. *By the second century one among each group of elders was clearly recognized as leader.*

Ignatius, for instance, wrote in A.D. 107 -

"It is clear that we must regard the episkopos (bishop) as the Lord himself" *(To the Ephesians, 6).*

"Be loyal to your *episkopos* (bishop) and to the *presbuteroi* (elders), and the *diakonoi* (deacons)" *(To the Philadephians, 7).*

"Follow your *episkopos*, every one of you, as obediently as Jesus Christ follows the Father. Obey your *presbuteroi* as you would the apostles. Give your *diakonoi* the same reverence that you would to a command from God" *(To Smyrna, 8).*

And Eusebius, quoting Cornelius of Rome in his comments on a well-known heretic (A.D. 250), writes -

"Thus he was unaware that there can be only one *episkopos* in a catholic church, in which as he knew perfectly well, there are 46 presbyters, 7 deacons, 7 sub-deacons, 42 attendants, 52 exorcists, readers and door-keepers and more than 1500 widows and distressed persons." (*History of the Church*, 6:43:8).

(This indicates that there were about 30,000 - 50,000 Christians in Rome at that time.)

Jerome (A.D. 377-420, in his *Letter to Evangelus*) wrote that "an *episkopos* is the same as a *presbuteros*;" but in most places a distinction was being drawn, so that the term *episkopos* was being used for the leader of the *presbuteroi*. (St. Jerome, *Letters and Select Works*, Eerdmans, 1979, pg. 288).

It is interesting to note from those quotations that the term *episkopos* was very early used to delineate the overall leader of a church, as distinct from the term *presbuteros*, which evidently applied to the next "rank." The term *poimen* (pastor), was hardly used at all!

It seems that the system prevailing in many churches today of a senior pastor, assisted by a team of pastors, and/or elders, is very similar to the

2nd century pattern - except for the use of the term "pastor" (*poimen*) rather than "bishop" (*episkopos*). [23]

2.7   THE AUTHORITY OF A PASTOR

It has already been noted that a pastor must avoid abusing his authority. The example of Jesus as the model pastor shows that the primary function is pastoral care, not correction.

Basically, a pastor may exercise authority only in two areas. These are -

a. *Doctrine (faith)*

He is responsible to teach the truth and to admonish those who teach error (Ac 20:28-30; 2 Ti 2:1-2, 14-26).

b. *Godly living (practice)*

He must preach and teach against sinful behavior and encourage godliness (Tit 1:10-16; 2:1-15; 3:1-2).

Beyond these two areas there is no biblical mandate for pastoral involvement. But within them he must speak with authority and without fear (Tit 2:15).

---

* **Think Spot**: *Is this a valid statement? "The danger in most churches is that they speak with too little authority; in some Pentecostal churches it is that they speak with too much."*

2.8   CAN A WOMAN BE A PASTOR?

As we have seen, women can certainly prophesy and share in pioneering ministry. There is probably no restriction on a woman being a pastor either; although there are some who argue that she may exercise a pastoral ministry only while she is herself under the authority of a male spiritual leader. See 1 Ti 2:11-12.

---

[23] Note that the "bishop" in Rome, during the time of Eusebius (as described above), must have held a position similar to that of an Anglican or Catholic bishop in our time. The leaders of large churches (like that at Rome) were slowly given authority over larger territories and wider groups of churches, and eventually the term "bishop" was reserved for those leaders alone - as it is in our day.

2.9 PASTORS AND OTHER MINISTRY GIFTS

It will be obvious that the lines of authority between a pastor and, say, an apostle, may well become tangled unless there is an understanding of their mutual ministries.

The answer seems to lie in He 13:17-18. Since it is the local church leaders who must give account of the flock, and who are responsible to feed the flock, they must also have the ultimate right to decide who ministers to it.

If they are wise, however, they will both recognize the other ministry-gifts to the Body of Christ and respect their contribution to the growth of the local church.

Note, too, how Paul (for instance) claims special rights as the "father" of the Corinthian church (1 Co 4:15) - but he also commends local leaders (1 Th 5:12- 13). This seems a godly balance.

On a practical basis, this means that itinerant ministries should deal with each local church only through its leaders - and that such leaders should show genuine hospitality to such ministries.

3. THE MINISTRY OF A TEACHER

Etymology:

didaskalos	= teacher, instructor (57 times in N.T.)
from *didaskein*	= to teach (97 times in N.T.)

Compare also -

didache	= teaching, doctrine (29 times)
didaskalia	= teaching, doctrine (21 times)

A teacher is simply one who teaches.

3.1 THE IMPORTANCE OF TEACHING

Teaching is greatly esteemed in the New Testament. For example, Jesus is called "Teacher" 42 times in the gospels. And Paul carefully places the three ministries of apostle, prophet and teacher above the gifts of miracles, tongues, etc. (1 Co 12:28 - *"Firstly ... secondly ... thirdly ..."*). In the great commission, Jesus instructed his disciples to *"teach"* people to obey all his commands (Mt 28:20).

Timothy and Titus are told over and again to teach their people (2 Ti 2:2, 24-25; Tit 2:1 ff), and that sound doctrine (i.e. teaching) is of prime importance (Tit 2:1; Ac 2:42; Ro 6:17; 16:17; He 13:9).

3.2   WHAT IS THE RELATION OF THE TEACHER TO OTHER MINISTRY GIFTS?

As noted above, the Greek grammar of Ep 4:11 suggests that *"pastors and teachers"* form one ministry. Similarly, Paul refers to himself as an *"apostle and teacher"* (1 Ti 2:7; 2 Ti 1:11). Through prophecy also, people may be instructed (1 Co 14:31) and evangelism clearly needs a teaching content (Ac 4:2; 5:21, 25, 28; etc.).

Teaching is thus fundamental to all ministry gifts. However, just as *"all may prophesy"* (1 Co 14:31) without being prophets, so all may teach (He 5:12) without being teachers. A specialist teaching ministry is one of the growth gifts - and needed as much as any of the others.

3.3   JESUS - THE MODEL TEACHER

Jesus is the model teacher. To analyze the content of his teaching would be a study in its own right, so we shall look briefly only at his teaching function.

a. *His teaching was unique and authoritative* (Jn 3:2; Mt 5:21 ff)

While no other teacher can speak with the unique authority of Jesus, the Christian teacher can nonetheless speak with the authority of the word of God - and indeed should do so (1 Ti 4:11 - *"command and teach ..."* Ac 4:13, 29, 31; 6:10).

b. *His teaching was Scripture-based*

Jesus often used Old Testament passages as a basis for his teaching (Lu 4:16 ff; Mt 5:21 ff; 15:3 ff). This is even more true of the Christian teacher who should be an expositor of the word.

c. *His teaching was colorful and illustrative*

Jesus used parables and stories (Mt 13:3, 10 ff; Mk 4:2; etc.), and colorful expressions (Mt 7:3- 6; 7:13-14) - a model to be followed by teachers today - especially in a TV-trained generation. It is important to speak in language that people understand.

d. *His teaching was practical*

Jesus said much about human relations (*Sermon on the Mount*), and everyday living (Mt 18:15-20; 19:1-12; Jn 15:9-17). This kind of teaching is always needed. It not only tells "why" but also "how."

e. *He gathered students around him* (Mt 10:1 ff)

In this sense, Jesus was fulfilling the accepted Jewish pattern for a teacher (cp. John the Baptist - Jn 1:35; Mt 11:2 ff). The fact that men gathered around him was the ultimate factor in his being recognized as a teacher (Kittel. Vol. II, pg. 153).

Of course, it goes without saying that a teacher must have someone to teach! But in this case, we see not just people in general being taught, but students specifically assembled together to learn. ("Disciple" = *mathetes* from *manthanein* = "to learn.") A similar pattern may well occur with specialist teachers today. (Note: with Jesus' disciples, this was a relatively short-term program, culminating in their also becoming teachers/evangelists, etc.)

f. *His disciples helped and supported him materially*

They went to buy food at Sychar (Jn 4:8); Judas was *"treasurer"* (Jn 13:29); Peter tried to defend Jesus (Jn 18:10) and so on. See also Mk 4:35 ff; 5:37 ff; 11:1 ff; Mt 26:17 ff. This again was typical of Jewish teacher-student relations - "a pupil (was) to do for his teacher all the things that a slave would do for his master" (Kittel, Vol. II, pg. 154).

It seems proper that teaching ministry should be supported by those who come to learn.

3.4 THE FUNCTION OF TEACHERS IN THE NEW TESTAMENT

The New Testament tells us little about the function of teachers in the early church.

a. *Teachers were "resident" in some local churches*

There were prophets and teachers at Antioch (Ac 13:1) and pastors and elders were often teachers (1 Ti 5:17).

b. *Some teachers were itinerant*

So Barnabas and Saul, two of those from Antioch became itinerant teachers (Ac 18:11) - and eventually apostles. The fact that false teachers went to Antioch from Judea (Ac 15:1) suggests that true teachers also moved among the churches. Apollos was an itinerant teacher (Ac 18:24 ff).

3.5   APOLLOS AS A MODEL TEACHER

a. *He had a thorough knowledge of the scriptures* (Ac 18:24)

So must all teachers be skilled in the Word.

b. *He was fervent and enthusiastic* (Ac 18:25)

Enthusiasm for the subject taught is infectious.

c. *He taught accurately* (Ac 18:25)

He was not content with half-truths.

d. *He was himself willing to learn* (Ac 18:26)

Every teacher must also be a student.

e. *He was courageous*

- not afraid to face those who disagreed (Ac 18:21).

f. *His teaching was "helpful"* (Ac 18:27)

Theoretical teaching that does not help in everyday, practical living is of little value to most believers.

g. *He was skilled in the use of scripture* (Ac 18:28)

Knowing the Word is one thing, but teaching it skillfully is another.

h. *He was not tied to one place* (Ac 28:24, 27)

He ministered to "the whole body" as far as this was practicable.

i. *He wanted the seed planted by the evangelist* (1 Co 3:6)

Here is an example of two ministry gifts in co-operation.

j. *He was neither greater nor less than other ministries* (1 Co 3:5-9; 16:12)

While all ministries are not the same in nature or influence, all are of equal standing before God.

---

*   **Think Spot**: *Ponder the support and following given to "name" ministries today. Advantages and disadvantages.*

k. *He was supported materially by the churches* (1 Ti 3:13-14)

All true ministry is worthy of support, whether permanently in a local church or not.

l. *He was firm in his convictions, yet responsible* (1 Co 16:12).

These points suggest a good basic model for teachers to follow today. (Note: Timothy is another New Testament teacher who could be considered as a model. So also is Paul.)

3.6 CAN A WOMAN BE A TEACHER?

At first sight, Paul's words in 1 Ti 2:12 might seem to rule this out. [24] Yet there may still be areas in which a woman may teach; for example:

teaching other women (Tit 2:3 ff)

teaching with her husband (Ac 18:26)

teaching privately (Ac 18:26)

There are also several references to women who *"worked hard in the Lord"* (Ro 16:4, 12). Although the nature of this work is not known, it is not unlikely that it included some form of teaching and/or instruction. (See also my comments in paragraph 2.5 above: "Can a woman be an apostle?")

4. MINISTRY GIFTS AND NATURAL GIFTS

The extent to which growth gifts and natural gifts overlap is unclear. Unlike the spiritual gifts of 1 Co 12:8-11, all of which are clearly attributed to the Holy Spirit's power, growth-gifts may well include natural talents. A good evangelist, for example, would probably also be a good salesman. A good teacher would be a good teacher anywhere.

However, there are clearly supernatural elements involved. The evangelist (for example) cannot bring about new birth; he cannot work

---

[24] Some argue that Paul's restriction here was based on contemporary social and cultural mores, and that the basic principle involved is only that of not giving unnecessary offense, and perhaps also the principle of maintaining proper order. In other words, 1 Ti 2:12 is akin in spirit to the injunction that women should be veiled when they worship (1 Co 11:1-16). Both injunctions contain a principle of decency and order which must be worked out differently in each different situation. In Paul's day, that meant women should be veiled and accept certain other restraints. In our culture, those rules may no longer be a valid outworking of the principle.
- Editor.

miracles without supernatural aid. Thus Ro 12:3 ff tells all who are gifted with some ministry to exercise their ministry by faith, so that it ever increases. See also Cl 4:17. No ministry is automatic - it only ever operates by faith initiative. (Note: this area of faith initiative could be developed much more, but it is really another subject.)

5.   GENERAL SUMMARY

A study of the ministry gifts makes it clear that they have a vital and enduring role in the Body of Christ, and in the family of God, to promote growth and maturity -

5.1   MINISTRY-GIFTS ARE ESSENTIAL

They are given to enable God's family to develop to maturity. Without them we will continue in ignorance, immaturity, and disunity.

5.2   SPIRITUAL GROWTH IS THE STANDARD

- by which the validity of such gifts may be measured. Thus the true can be distinguished from the false. Any gift or ministry which fails to produce the requisite growth must be either false, or in some way faulty.

Furthermore, where there is growth, even if there are aspects of such ministries that are unusual or different or even questioned, these should be treated generously, and with love, for the sake of the ultimate benefits.

Thus we will be no longer children fighting over toys, but mature adults recognizing true value and real benefit to God's family whenever it occurs.

5.3   GROWTH-GIFTS PROVIDE AN INTEGRATING FACTOR

- that binds churches together in unity. Where organization fails, divinely-bestowed ministry-gifts may succeed in helping to bind God's greater family together. Theirs is a ministry of integration or wholeness (the Latin word integer means "whole").

5.4   THERE IS A GREAT NEED

- for those who are apostles, prophets, evangelists, pastors and teachers to exercise their ministries by faith. Many such ministries are possibly dormant, or locked into churches or church organizations, when they should be free to express themselves. Such people need to move in faith, taking the initiative and exercising their gifts (Ro 12:3 ff).

May God grant more and more such growth gifts to his church today! (Mt 9:36-38).

6.   APPENDIX

Timothy and Titus have both been used in this lesson as examples of pastors, teachers, prophets, etc. What, in fact, were they?

First of all, it needs to be noted again that the ministry gifts overlap to some extent. For instance, one may be a teacher-prophet, or evangelist-teacher, or apostle- prophet, etc.

This seems to have been the case with Timothy and Titus. Consider the following points about each:

6.1   TIMOTHY

a. He is called Paul's *"true child"* (1 Ti 1:2) and *"my son"* (1:18; 2:1)

b. He was gifted with spiritual gifts (1 Ti 1:18; 4:14; 2 Ti 1:6-7)

c. He was a teacher (1 Ti 4:11-13; 6:2 b; 2 Ti 2:2; 4:2)

d. He was an evangelist (2 Ti 4:5)

e. He was Paul's companion in ministry (Ac 17:14-15; 18;5; 19:22; 20:4; Ro 16:21; 1 Co 4:17; 2 Co 1:1; Ph 1;1; etc.)

f. He was in charge of the church at Ephesus (1 Ti 1:3 ff) and set it in order (3:11; 4:11 ff)

g. His time at Ephesus was, however, apparently only temporary (1 Ti 3:15; 4:13)

h. There were already elders at Ephesus (Ac 20:17 ff) - apparently Timothy was in authority over them

i. Tradition has it that Timothy was the bishop (*episkopos*) at Ephesus (Eusebius, *Church History*, III, 4)

CONCLUSION: Timothy was actually an apostle, who exercised other gifts as needed.

6.2   TITUS

a. He is called Paul's *"partner and fellow worker"* (= apostle?; 2 Co 8:16-28)

b. He is also called Paul's *"true child in the faith"* (Ti 1:4)

c. He set in order the church in Crete (1:5)

d. He was a teacher (2:1; 3:1; etc.)

e. Tradition has it that he was bishop (*episkopos*) of the churches in Crete (Eusebius, *Church History*, III.4).

CONCLUSION: he was an apostle who exercised other gifts as needed.

LESSON FIVE

BISHOPS, DEACONS, AND OTHERS

1. BACKGROUND

The question of how a local church should be organized has been a matter of great debate for many centuries.

There have been three major schools of thought. They may be broadly classified as -

> *Episcopal*
>
> *Congregational*
>
> *Presbyterian*

1.1 EPISCOPAL

The *Episcopal* system stems originally from the concept of apostolic authority. This authority is seen as having been now transferred to the *episkopos* (bishop/overseer). Historical evidence for this may be readily found in the writings of people as early as Clement (A.D. 96) in his letter to the *Corinthians* (par. 40), and Ignatius (A.D. 107) in his letters to the *Magnesians* (par. 6) and the *Thrallians* (par. 3).

It is more fully developed in later writers like Irenaeus, Eusebius, and Jerome. The latter, for instance, says that bishops and elders should take the apostles and their companions as examples because *"they hold the rank which these once held"* (To *Paulinus*, 5); he even goes so far as to say that bishops, presbyters, and deacons occupy in the church *"the same position as those which were occupied by Aaron, his sons, and the Levites in the temple"* (To *Evangelus*).

The Catholic church became the most fully developed example of Episcopal government, with the pope being the supreme authority. Basically, any church organization which has a bishop (or some similar official) in authority over a group of churches may be described as Episcopal. Some other examples are the Anglican Church, the Orthodox churches, the Episcopalian Church, and to a varying degree some Methodist and Lutheran churches.

The Apostolic Church, a Pentecostal group, emphasizes the authority of apostolic ministry and thus has an organization similar in concept to the Episcopalian.

The Salvation Army is, in its own way, a kind of Episcopal organization - but for quite different reasons! (And they would reject the term Episcopal.)

1.2 Congregational

As its name suggests, the *Congregational* system allows each local church to be self-governing. It stresses the freedom and autonomy of local churches and sees final authority as being vested in the congregation itself.

Although freely recognizing the historical antecedents of the Episcopal system, most Congregationalists feel that the Fathers quoted above were departing from the First Century pattern and that the New Testament teaches congregational autonomy.

Baptists, Congregationalists and some Pentecostals are examples of churches which practice congregational government.

Although such churches may get together in denominational groupings of various kinds, final decision-making about all matters of policy is vested in the congregation itself.

1.3 Presbyterian

Presbyterian organization also sees local church autonomy as the biblical pattern. But it sees leadership and government as being in the hands of the presbyters (or, elders). Each church has its own elders. In addition to this, however, the ministers and/or other local church leaders may meet together as a senior presbytery which deals with overall policy, especially the placement of ministers.

The Presbyterian Church, the Reformed Churches, the Uniting Church, are examples of denominations with some form of Presbyterian organization.

In this section we shall try to establish what was done in New Testament days. But it should be remembered that it may be impossible to do this with finality - some aspects must, of necessity, be left open.

And we should also remember that principles of growth and expansion do not really depend on the kind of organization employed so much as on the ministry-gifts that function, the preaching of the word, and other factors (which will be developed in a later section).

In other words, while it is important to use biblical patterns of organization wherever possible, the vital thing to remember is that revival does not depend on these - it can occur in any church, regardless of its structure!

2. MEMBERSHIP

As we have seen already, the local church was a visible organization. Therefore, membership was tangible and discernible.

It is clearly not enough to say that you are a Christian but that you don't belong to a church. Or, that you belong to the universal church, but not the local church.

To be a Christian is to be a member of Christ's body - and that body is expressed through local groups of believers.

2.1 MEMBERSHIP IMPLIES A RECOGNITION OF THE NEED FOR -

a. *Fellowship*. Believers are expected to meet together (He 10:25). The church, by definition, is a "meeting" or "assembly" of God's people.

b. *Leadership*. Believers are enjoined to respect and obey their leaders (1 Th 5:12-13; He 13:7, 17). This is clearly impossible if one is not part of a church nor in some practical and realistic way subject to its leadership.

c. *Discipline*. The most severe form of New Testament discipline was to cut people off from fellowship (Mt 18:17; 1 Co 5:5; 2 Co 2:5-11). This is obviously no problem to those who are already out of fellowship!

This kind of discipline also presupposes some form of *membership*.

d. *Commitment*. Believers are expected to be committed to both Christ and his church. The various analogies of the church imply a committed and stable membership -

the body - we are all members committed to each other (Ro 12:5; Ep 5:30).

the temple - bricks must be firmly in place! (Ep 2:21; 1 Pe 2:5).

the family - members of a family do not "come and go" (Ep 2:20-21).

the field - the grain is committed to the ground (Jn 12:24-25).

the bride - the whole of a bride's body is committed to her husband (Ep 5:31-32; 1 Co 7:4).

2.2 THE NORMAL NEW TESTAMENT PATTERN FOR ENTRY INTO THE CHURCH WAS REPENTANCE, FAITH AND BAPTISM

Those who followed this pattern at Pentecost were considered as being added to the church (Ac 2:41, 47). Paul also points out that by one Spirit we are baptized into one body (1 Co 12:13).

So we see that the Spirit brings us into the body, but by the outward act of baptism we respond to this.

2.3 CONCLUSION

It is plain that membership of the church in New Testament days was clear and specific.

Unfortunately the contemporary idea that you can be a church member without attending church, or that church membership, once decided, is more or less permanent, regardless of what happens, is very popular. It is also very misleading.

Membership is for those who have repented of their sins, confessed their faith in Christ and been baptized. It is an act of commitment to Christ and his body on earth. It is for all true believers.

3. GOVERNMENT

3.1 NEW TESTAMENT LOCAL CHURCHES WERE GOVERNED BY ELDERS

The churches at Jerusalem and Antioch were both ruled by elders (Ac 15:6 ff; 11:30). Paul and Barnabas appointed elders in each of the new churches they established (Ac 14:23). The Ephesian church was clearly led by elders (Ac 20:17 ff). Paul's letter to Timothy makes specific reference to elders governing the church (1 Ti 5:17). And Peter calls on elders to rule wisely and patiently (1 Pe 5:1-4).

3.2   THE TERMS ELDER, BISHOP AND PASTOR ARE SYNONYMOUS

a. *Elder*

Etymology:

presbuteros:

- old, aged (Ac 2:17; 1 Ti 5:1)

- ancestor (Mt 15:2; He 11:2)

- title of honor among the Jews (Mt 16:21; Ac 4:8; etc.)

- elder of the congregation (Ac 11:30; 20:17; Ja 5:14; etc.)

- one of 24 in the heavenly assembly (Re 4:4)

(used 67 times in the N.T.).

presbuterion: elders as a group (e.g. 1 Ti 4:14).

(used 3 times in the N.T.)

presbutes: old man (used 3 times in the N.T.)

presbutis: old woman (used once in the N.T.)

The word *presbuteros* is clearly related to the concept of seniority in terms of age. But it is also clear that elders were also those among the aged who were in positions of authority. (Every *presbutes* was not necessarily a *presbuteros*.)

b. *Bishop*

The word *episkopos* is a synonym for *presbuteros*.

Etymology:

episkopos: overseer, ruler, supervisor, bishop

(used 5 times in the N.T.)

episkopeo: take oversight

(used twice in the N.T.)

episkope: office of bishop

(used 3 times in the N.T.)

c. *Pastor*

Etymology:

poimen: shepherd

> (18 times in the N.T., 13 of which refer to Christ)

poimaino: I shepherd, I tend, I care for, I rule

> (11 times in the N.T.)

poimne: flock, herd

> (5 times in the N.T.)

poimnion: little flock

> (5 times in the N.T.)

That the terms *presbuteros*, *episkopos* and *poimen* are synonymous is obvious from a simple comparison of scriptures:

First, it is obvious that a pastor's task is to *shepherd*, for that is what the word "pastor" means ("pastor" is simply the Latin word for "shepherd").

Paul, however, tells the elders (*presbuteros*) at Ephesus that it is their task to guard themselves and "all the flock" (*poimnion*) over which God's spirit has made them overseers (*episkopos*). He then goes on to tell them to "shepherd" or "tend" (*poimaino*) the church (Ac 20:17, 28).

That passage alone clearly establishes that "elder," "overseer/bishop," and "pastor," are all descriptions of the same ministry. Similarly, had bishops, elders or pastors been different people, Paul would hardly have ignored some of them in greetings, such as Ph 1:1.

The point is further established in 1 Pe 2:25, where Jesus is spoken of as both shepherd (*poimen*) and overseer (*episkopos*) of our souls; and in 1 Pe 5:1 ff, where Peter instructs the elders (*presbuteros*) to "be shepherds" (*poimaino*) of the flock (*poimnion*) of God. He then refers to them "serving as overseers" (*episkopeo*). Then he makes further references to both "the flock" (*poimnion*) and "the chief shepherd" (*archipoimen*).

Finally, the description of the qualifications for an overseer (*episkopos*) given in 1 Ti 3:1 ff are almost identical to those given for an elder (*presbuteros*) in Tit 1:6 ff - further evidence of the similarity between the two terms.

We can probably also add -

> *hegoumenos* = ruler
>
> *kubernesis* = administrator

- as further synonyms for "overseer." So the believers addressed in the letter to the Hebrews are urged to obey their leaders (*hegoumenos*) in the same way that other believers are expected to obey elders (1 Ti 3:1 ff). Further, Jesus is spoken of as both shepherd (*poimaino*) and ruler (*hegoumenos*) of Israel (Mt 2:6). And governing ability (*kubernesis*) is listed as one of the skills that God has appointed in the church (1 Co 12:28) - probably a reference to the work of an overseer or elder.

Evidence from the patristic writings also suggests that the terms *episkopos* and *presbuteros* are synonymous. Clement (AD 96) uses the terms interchangeably (*To the Corinthians*, 42-44); and Jerome clearly states: "the apostle (Paul) teaches that elders are the same as bishops" (*To Evangelus*, 1).

"Chalice of Antioch" 4th or 5th century.

To summarize, we may say that all the terms discussed so far refer to the same office, the different expressions being used simply to emphasize different aspects of the work involved. See the following chart - [25]

Greek Term	English Translation	Aspect of Ministry Emphasized
presbuteros	elder	seniority, wisdom, experience, care
episkopos	overseer, bishop	supervision, direction
poimen	shepherd, pastor	care, teaching
hegoumenos	leader	leadership
kubernesis	governor	governing skills

4. HISTORICAL BACKGROUND

To understand fully the concept behind New Testament church government we need to familiarize ourselves with the cultural background of the church.

4.1 ELDER

The concept of eldership was very ancient. Most of the peoples in the ancient world had recognized elders. These were usually the older, and hence wiser and more experienced, men of the community. There were elders among the Egyptians (Ge 50:7), the Moabites and Midianites (Nu 22:7), the Greeks, and the Hebrews.

Moses set aside seventy elders to assist him (Nu 11:16 ff). Later, elders discharged the duties of local authorities (De 19:12; 21:2; Js 20:4; Jg 8:14; etc.). Although numbers varied, they were often a sizable group (e.g. 77 in Gideon's day - Jg 8:14). By the time of Samuel, the elders were instrumental in the setting up of a king (1 Sa 8:4), and were later involved in monarchial affairs (1 Sa 30:26; 2 Sa 3:17; 1 Kg 21:8-11). The elders of a city acted as judges (De 22:15). They exercised leadership after the exile (Ezr 5:5, 9; etc.).

It is noteworthy that the leaders basically acted as a representative group for the people. There was normally one strong leader - a "judge,"

---

[25] Note: the differences emphasized here are less important than the overall similarities between the five terms.

prophet, priest or king - who was above the elders, but who was often influenced by them.

By the time of Christ, the elders of the Jews had adopted a strongly religious identity. This was inevitable, for civil power now resided in the hands of the Romans.

This new aspect of authority was exercised mainly through the synagogue and the sanhedrin.

The *synagogue* was essentially a place of worship and teaching - but not of sacrifice. Hence, it was led, not by priests, but by rabbis, or teachers - usually older men or elders.

The *sanhedrin* probably developed from a council of elders (cp. Pr 31:23). By Jesus' day it included both priests and elders (Mt 21:23; 26:3; 26:47; Mk 11:27; Ac 4:5; 6:12; etc.). It was the supreme governing body for the Jews.

It is interesting to note that in some other countries the elders had also assumed a greater religious authority (e.g. Egypt, Asia Minor).

In summary, elders were senior men who had authority at local level, and who represented all the people as a group. A king, "judge," or prophet, however, might still have a greater authority than the elders.

4.2   OVERSEER

The word *episkopos* was used to describe what the person concerned *did* rather than what he *was*; that is, function rather than office.

Among the Greeks, for instance, overseers were sent to regulate new colonies or to act as municipal officers. In Rhodes, there was a council of five overseers, and the temple there had an *episkopos*.

In summary, we can simply assume that the term "overseer" had a very general meaning, just as it does in modern English, and could be applied to any position of leadership, government, etc.

4.3   PASTOR

The term "pastor" needs no further discussion - its simple meaning of shepherd is sufficient background, and this is fully described in John 10.

Again, in the New Testament this word describes function rather than office.

5.   THE ROLE OF ELDERS/OVERSEERS/PASTORS

From our knowledge of the cultural background, and our study of the New Testament it is possible to form a fairly comprehensive and composite picture of government in the New Testament church.

5.1   PLURAL ELDERSHIP

It would appear that the early church adopted some of the synagogue patterns of organization and worship (see below under "worship"). Hence, the concept of eldership was probably modeled fairly closely on the synagogue concept.

No doubt the eldership pattern in local communities was also followed. In fact, it has been suggested that the elders chosen in a local church may actually have been those who were already elders in the community, and hence respected by the people before they were even appointed.

In either case, this would presuppose a plurality of elders in each local church. The New Testament itself indicates this, as the word often occurs in the plural, especially when used in reference to elders themselves, rather than in reference to the position or responsibility of an elder. See Ac 14:23; 15:2, 4, 6, 22-23; 16:4; 20:17; 21:18; Ph 1:1; 1 Ti 5:17; Ja 5:14; 1 Pe 5:1; He 13:7, 17.

5.2   SINGLE LEADERSHIP

Over and above eldership, comes the ministry of an apostle. This is obvious from the letters of Paul, for instance, who has no hesitation in writing to churches where there was an eldership, and giving them clear and specific teaching and instructions.

Similarly, both Timothy and Titus are set in charge of churches, with a mandate above that of the local elders.

What is not clear is whether the churches at Ephesus and Crete were single congregations with elderships, or groups of congregations, with elders in each. Titus 1:5 suggests the latter. If so, then this reflects the position in Israel, where a king or "judge" gave single leadership to a nation composed of tribes and communities which had their own local church leaders (elders).

While apostolic ministry was still recognized, such a position was acceptable and workable. With the turn of the century, however, the use of the term "apostle" became less frequent. It occurs in *The Didache* (c 160 AD) but rarely elsewhere. More frequently we see apostolic authority being accorded to one of the local officials.

To differentiate between him and the rest of the elders, he was called the *episkopos*, while the rest continued to be called *presbuteroi*. Hence, the beginnings of the modern Episcopal system of church government.

Initially, the bishop was probably just the leader of the elders in a local congregation. The letters of Ignatius (AD. 107) indicate this. For instance -

> "Obey your elders too, as you would the apostles; give your deacons the same reverence that you would to a command from God. Make sure no step affecting the church is ever taken by anyone without the bishop's sanction. The sole Eucharist (i.e. thanksgiving) you should consider valid is one that is celebrated by the bishop himself, or by some person authorized by him ... Nor is it permissible to conduct baptisms or love-feasts without the bishop ..." (*To the Smyrnaeans*, 8).

If the only valid baptism or communion was that conducted by a bishop, this would indicate that his was essentially a local church role - or at the most, a relatively small "parish" or group of churches.

So there is a simple pattern emerging which seems to have followed these stages (the larger boxes each represent a local church) -

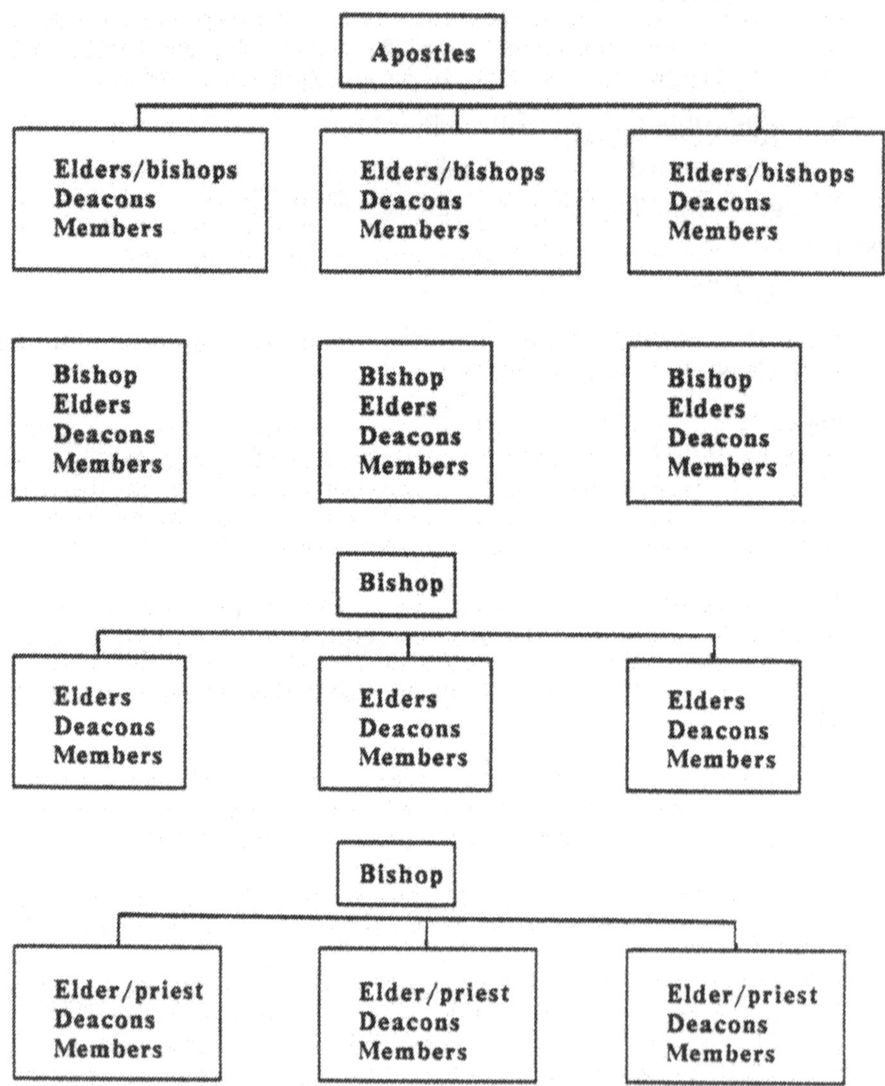

It can easily be seen how the Episcopal system thus developed.

A similar trend has developed in this century in many Pentecostal churches. Going back to the first century, and seeing only one basic leadership office (pastor/elder/overseer etc.), they have adopted a plural eldership with a single leader - however they have usually called this leader a "pastor" rather than a "bishop."

But there are also many various variations of this approach, including that of having both pastors and elders in the one local church, usually with one pastor as the senior pastor. (In this case, the "elders" probably correspond more nearly to New Testament deacons.)

5.3 THE DUTIES OF ELDERS

This can be summarized as follows:

> Pastoral care (Ac 20:28; 1 Pe 5:2; 1 Ti 3:5)
>
> Teaching (1 Ti 3:2; Tit 1:9)
>
> Administration (1 Ti 5:17-18; 1 Co 12:28)
>
> Oversight (1 Ti 3:1; Ac 20:28)
>
> Example (1 Pe 5:3)
>
> Ministry to the sick (Ja 5:14)
>
> Care of the needy (1 Ti 5:3 ff)
>
> Direction (1 Co 12:28; Ac 20:28)
>
> Correction and discipline (1 Th 5:12; He 13:17)
>
> Hospitality (Tit 1:8)
>
> Protection (Ac 20:28-31).

In simple terms, just as a shepherd attends to the physical welfare of his sheep, so a pastor must attend to the spiritual welfare of his people.

---

* **Think Spot**: *How necessary is it for every elder to be able to fulfill all the above requirements? (Consider the implications of 1 Ti 5:17-18, for instance. Also, the reasons for plurality of eldership).*

---

6. THE RELATIONSHIP BETWEEN LOCAL CHURCH LEADERS AND OTHER MINISTRY GIFTS

In this section, we are again forced to look at descriptive rather than prescriptive passages and then to attempt to relate them to the churches of today.

6.1 APOSTOLIC AUTHORITY

Even a cursory examination of the New Testament makes it clear that apostles had a recognized and accepted authority over local churches. Their letters, for instance, give obvious evidence of this -

Paul - 1 Co 5:5; 11:17; 2 Co 11:28; Ga 1:6 ff; Ph 2:12; 2 Th 3:6-15; 2 Pe 2:15-16

Peter - 1 Pe 2:13 ff; 3:1 ff; 5:1 ff; 2 Pe 3:1 ff.

John - 2 Jn 7 ff; 3 Jn 9 ff.

James - Ja 5:1 ff.

Jude - Jude 17 ff.

Of course, the very existence of these letters is sufficient evidence of apostolic authority.

In the case of Paul, he speaks very strongly to churches that he himself founded (e.g. Ga 1:6 ff; 2 Th 3:6-11); but even to churches he did not found, he gives specific instructions (e.g. Cl 4:1 ff).

Similarly, Paul and Barnabas appointed elders in the churches they established (Ac 14:23). Later Paul set both Timothy and Titus over the churches in Ephesus and Crete respectively.

It would appear that teachers also moved from church to church with a recognized and accepted right to teach, for example, Apollos (Ac 18:24 ff). Compare also the movements of "false teachers" (Ac 15:1 ff). No doubt prophets, too, were often itinerant (e.g. Judas and Silas - Ac 15:22, 32; Agabus and his fellow prophets - 11:26 ff; 21:10).

Such itinerant ministry was clearly an integrating factor between the churches and helped to keep them in a state of unity and awareness of one another's needs. Paul's role in organizing offerings for the suffering Christians in Judea is a clear example (1 Co 16:1 ff; 2 Co 8:16 ff).

When there was a dispute over law and grace at Antioch, the church appointed Paul and Barnabas (who were not yet recognized as "apostles") and some others to go to Jerusalem to consult the apostles there on the matter (Ac 15:1-4).

Finally, Paul's own statements are quite specific. He expects to be obeyed (Ph 2:12; 2 Th 3:14-15; 1 Co 14:37 ff; 2 Co 2:9). He describes the "care of all the churches" as his responsibility (2 Co 11:28).

6.2   PASTORAL AUTHORITY

Clearly, as we have seen, elders were given authority in the local church. The apostles themselves taught that the elders were to be obeyed in spiritual matters (He 13:7, 17; 1 Ti 3:5; 1 Pe 5:5).

Paul and Barnabas were sent out by the church at Antioch (Ac 13:1) and made a point of returning there (Ac 14:28; 18:22) whenever possible - evidently in recognition of their responsibility to do so.

Further, local leaders are answerable to God for the people under their care (He 13:17; Ja 3:1).

6.3 BALANCED AUTHORITY

The reconciling of these two areas of authority is not necessarily difficult.

a. As we have seen, local churches often had little practical control over other ministry gifts. Paul and his companions for instance, were away for years at a time from their home church.

b. On the other hand, it appears that itinerant ministries worked in co-operation with local leadership wherever possible. So in the matter of the offering for the Judean church, Paul goes out of his way to avoid criticism (2 Co 8:20-21) and freely co-operates with the Macedonian and Corinthian churches (2 Co 8:1 ff, especially vs. 18-19).

On other occasions, he pleads, rather than commands (1 Co 1:10; 1 Co 9:1 ff; Ro 12:1; Ph 4:2).

c. In the case of prophetic ministry, believers are urged to weigh it up and assess it, not to accept it uncritically (1 Co 14:29; 1 Th 5:20-21). As we have seen, prophets continued to be tested in the second century.

d. Authority of ministry can only go so far as people allow it to go. If they reject it, there is little that the person claiming the authority can do, except repeat his claims and restate his credentials (cp. 2 Co 10:8 ff).

In practical terms, this means that if an apostle or evangelist is visiting a church, the final authority in that church lies with the oversight. They are the ones who decide how far the authority of the visitor should go while he is there (cp. Ac 18:2).

e. All authority must be balanced by the authority of others. So Paul did return to his home church at Antioch, but on his second and third journeys he first reported to the church at Jerusalem (Ac 18:22; 21:17). So Paul had two points of reference: the elders at Antioch; the apostles at Jerusalem. He desired the endorsement and support of these other spiritual leaders, although he was prepared to stand alone with God if that were necessary.

Similarly, he points out how he specifically sought endorsement on other occasions as well (Ga 2:1 ff, especially vs. 6). Indeed there are dangers if individual ministries are not subject to others. This applies, in fact, to both itinerant and local ministries - their ultimate safeguard lies in their willingness to be subject to others (an excellent biblical principle, of course - Ep 5:21; Ph 2:1-5).

---

* **Think Spot**: *While the members of a church are to be subject to the oversight, to whom are the oversight subject? What if the "leader" of the elders is very strong and able to manipulate the rest? Where is his safety? Or, what of a very strong evangelist, or prophet? What does this tell us about the position of independent churches?*

6.4   SUMMARY

a. Ministry-gifts have an authority beyond that of individual churches.

b. Local leaders have final authority within the local church.

c. All authority is limited by the extent to which it is received.

d. There is safety in the mutual recognition of gifts.

---

* **Think Spot**: *In what ways do you think local churches have suffered in recent years by the failure of most denominations to acknowledge or recognize apostles, prophets, etc.?*

Illustration: An interesting example of mutual recognition of gifts may be seen in the Australian Christian Church, in Adelaide. This congregation of about 200 people (mainly Chinese) is under the guidance of a group of six elders, all of whom are professional people with full-time occupations. The elders take all the mid-week Bible studies, carry out personal care and administer the church. They call upon three men who are engaged in full-time teaching ministry to provide regular teaching input at the Sunday services.

Occasionally, other ministries (evangelist/prophet, etc.) are also used. The teachers are not normally involved in pastoral or administrative matters, although they are free to offer advice and help if they wish. In this way, local autonomy is preserved and local leadership is respected, while the benefit of other ministries is gained. Incidentally, this congregation uses a building owned by the Uniting Church, and structures service times to avoid clashing. Thus, very little money is tied up in property, etc., and they can give generously to missions and other causes.

It is an interesting example of a local church which probably comes very close to the New Testament pattern of organization.

Lesson Six

What About Denominations?

1.   Inter-Church Organization

There is no New Testament evidence of religious denominations. The New Testament speaks only of local churches or of the universal church. Does this mean that denominations are wrong?

1.1   Geographical Organization

New Testament churches were often grouped geographically; for example, *Galatia* (1 Co 16:1; Ga 1:1), *Macedonia* (2 Co 8:1), *Crete* (Tit 1:5), *Asia* (Re 1:11). Furthermore, these churches could obviously work together where necessary (2 Co 8:19, 23-24; 2 Co 9:2).

In the larger cities, each church may well have been, in practice, a group of smaller churches, meeting in homes, and perhaps occasionally getting together as a large group (e.g. Ro 16:5; Phm 2). Organization was, again, largely geographical.

Note: the Swedish Pentecostal churches follow this pattern. One "church" (e.g. the 7,000 member Filadelfia Church) may actually have up to 25 meeting places, all used concurrently. Each group has its own pastor, but all pastors meet together as a common oversight.

1.2   Apostolic Integration

There is also evidence of churches co-operating together as the result of integrating activity by apostles; for example, in the matter of sending aid to Jerusalem (2 Co 8:16 ff; Ph 4:14 ff).

Indeed, this aspect of apostolic ministry is one which is often overlooked, but which is very significant - although even here there are dangers, as there were at Corinth, with small groups (perhaps house churches) lining up behind individual leader (1 Co 1:10 ff). That practice is of course roundly condemned by Paul.

1.3   Fraternal Interest

It is probably fair to suggest that some churches formed a relationship on a fraternal basis, based on common interest and/or brotherly love, as well as on geographical proximity. So the churches at Jerusalem and Antioch seem to have shared much in common (cp. Ac 15), although other churches (e.g. Samaria) were nearer to them geographically.

1.4   Local Autonomy

Beyond these three areas, however, there is no New Testament evidence of organization between churches. Notice that when Christ addressed the seven church of Asia (Re 1:11; 2:1 ff), he spoke to each individually and related to each directly.

Each local church has its own leadership and must be responsible for its own vision and program.

1.5   Historical Developments

It is in the second and third centuries that we see more obvious groupings of churches occurring. At first, this was basically geographic. Very soon, however, it became doctrinal. One of the early conflicts was actually a combination of both. The churches in Asia were keeping a different Easter date (in their case, following the Passover) from the rest of the churches, a fact which caused a lively debate between "camps" (see Eusebius, H.E., 5.23).

But there were also heretical; or deviant groups who gathered people to themselves - such as the Ebionites, Gnosticism, the Montanists, Monarchianism, Arianism, and so on.

This was the real origin of denominationalism - the grouping of churches and people on the basis of doctrinal emphasis, rather than on the basis of love and allegiance to Christ. [26]

1.6   Conclusions

a. It is possible for autonomous local churches to co-exist in fellowship. The Swedish Pentecostal churches have successfully done so. There is no national constitution, for instance, and no appointed national leader. But 100,000 people and over 500 local churches are all members

---

[26] But see also 1.6.e, next page.

of just one Pentecostal movement. This seems to be very close to the New Testament paradigm.

b. Autonomous churches can work together on a fraternal basis. Indeed, they need to do so. The leaders of churches should meet together for their own protection and encouragement. Autonomy does not mean isolation or independence.

Similarly, itinerant ministries need the protection of fellowship with others.

c. Autonomous churches can co-operate in united ventures. There is no reason why local churches should not join together in co-operative ventures, to support missionaries to publish books, to establish a Bible College, etc. (Again cp. 2 Co 8:16 ff).

One local church could also act as an agent or administrative office for the rest (which is also good economy).

This is wise stewardship and use of resources.

d. Any local church can enjoy a direct relationship with the Lord Jesus Christ. Churches that belong to more structured denominations need not be prevented by that from enjoying a direct relationship with Christ (as in Revelation ch 1-3).

The function of ministry gifts, the use of spiritual gifts, successful outreach, evangelism, pastoral care, etc., can all take place in any system. The important thing is to have correct attitudes, aggressive faith, good leadership, and a joyful love - and above all, to be in such a relationship with Christ that you clearly hear what the Spirit is saying to the church!

e. I ask you to remember especially that the New Testament does not *prescribe* how churches should be set up; it only *describes* what was done in the first century. I have presented one point of view in this chapter. Obviously, others would argue equally strongly for an Episcopal or congregational approach. In contrast with my comment in 7.5 above, some would argue that important traditional, historical, political, and cultural factors also lie behind the formation of many of the major denominations. An exhaustive study of the subject would also raise such questions as

- how far is the New Testament paradigm binding on modern church structures?

- how much (if any) of the modern denominational structures represents the will of God for the church today?

- how much (if any) of the formation of church tradition was a product of the Holy Spirit guiding the church into changing patterns to suit changing conditions?

- could the modern church continue to function world-wide, or would it disintegrate, if the New Testament paradigm were universally embraced?

- would the work of the church be enhanced by forming one super denomination, or by scrapping all denominations, or by reorganizing into strictly regional denominations?

- should doctrinal differences be minimized, or more strictly defined?

- is it possible or necessary, or even desirable, to effect any meaningful change in the present situation? Can high church and low church ever meet happily?

- and so on.

Clearly, those who favor denominational structures, and those who view them with disfavor, will give different answers to those questions. It should be noted, though, that the answers (if there are any) can hardly come from the New Testament, but must be drawn from other, non-biblical, sources. For that reason, in my analysis above, I have tried to keep close to the New Testament, and to present the data it contains as fairly and as impartially as I can. The main point is that the *structures* are really less significant than the *ministry*. Where there is Christ-given leadership and ministry, the local church can flourish, regardless of its structure, or the structure of any movement to which it may belong.

2.   APPOINTMENT TO OFFICE

Churches and denominations differ strongly, at times, about how people should be appointed to office. The major reason for this probably lies in the fact that the New Testament actually describes several different methods, which were used at different times and different places, and we have fallen into the usual trap of trying to make a given method the norm! (This is a clear example of the dangers of taking descriptive passages as prescriptive.)

Consider the following points:

2.1 ALL MINISTRY IS GOD-GIVEN

Before any ministry, ability or gift can be recognized by man, it must first be implanted by God.

If there is God-given ministry or ability present, the most that we can do is to provide training, encouragement, and recognition, to help it to function better. If there is no such divine gift present, it doesn't matter how much training, encouragement, or recognition we give; that person's ministry will never develop effectively. This point has been clearly established already.

> * **Think Spot**: *Assess the place of theological schools and Bible colleges in the light of this.*

2.2 METHODS OF APPOINTMENT SEEM TO BE RELATIVE TO THE NATURE OF THE MINISTRY CONCERNED

When we examine the New Testament, we find that there were times when there was a definite calling and commissioning by the Holy Spirit. There were other occasions when very ordinary, or natural, methods were used.

So Matthias was chosen by lot (Ac 1:15-26); Paul and Barnabas through prophecy (Ac 13:1 ff); Luke by selection of the churches (2 Co 8:19); the Asian elders by the apostles (Ac 14:23); and so on. It does seem possible, however, to categorize New Testament methods of appointment to some extent - largely by reference to the kind of ministry involved. The choice of an apostle, for instance, seems to have been made differently from that of an elder or ambassador.

2.3 APPOINTMENT OF APOSTLES

a. *Matthias was chosen*

- on the basis of certain pre- requisites (namely, that he had known Jesus' ministry first- hand, and that he had borne witness to the resurrection - Ac 1:22 ff)

- through nomination (vs. 23)

- through prayer (vs. 24)

- through the drawing of lots (vs. 26)

An ornamented container in which
incense is burned. Called a "censer".

In this case, two men fulfilled the prerequisites. So the believers prayed, in faith, that God would direct the drawing of lots.

This method is never again referred to in the New Testament. It is interesting that it was used before the outpouring of the Spirit at Pentecost. May it therefore be inferred that it was not needed thereafter?

Note: The drawing or casting of lots was a common Old Testament practice. See 1 Ch 24:5; Nu 26:55; Js 15:1 ff; 1 Sa 14:41-42; Js 7:16-18. The Urim and the Thummin may also have been a kind of lot (see Ex 28:30; Le 8:8; De 33:8; 1 Sa 23:6-14; 28:6). Drawing of lots was done in trust in the sovereignty of God - that he would control the result (Pr 16:33).

The most common method was that of writing the names of the persons on pieces of stone, and the names of the offices, etc., on other pieces. Stones were then drawn until a result was achieved. We do not know what method was used in the case of Matthias.

b. *Paul and Barnabas*

Paul and Barnabas received a direct commission by the Holy Spirit (Ac 13:1-3). This was probably through a word of prophecy - as indicated by the connection between verses 1a and 2a.

Note, however, that the church then prayed and fasted before sending them - possibly to confirm the call? Then, they laid hands on them. In summary, we see three steps:

>-direct call of God

>-confirmed in prayer by the church

>-endorsed by laying on of hands.

At no point, however, are we told that Paul and Barnabas were actually "appointed" apostles. Their recognition seems to have come more from the effectiveness of their ministry. Certainly, it is to this that Paul later appeals for his credentials (2 Co 12:11-12; Ga 1:11 ff).

c. *Peter*

Peter, of course, was automatically recognized as an apostle - having been chosen by Jesus as one of his disciples.

His first apostolic ministry to the Gentiles, however, resulted from yet another divine call (Ac 10:9-23). Although this call could not be immediately endorsed by the church (there was no-one else present), it was reinforced by the arrival of emissaries from Cornelius. It was also later confirmed by the results that attended Peter's ministry to Cornelius (10:44-48), and later again by the church at Jerusalem (11:18).

So we see:

>- a divine call

>- confirmed by circumstances, by its effective outworking,

and by the approval of the church.

d. *James*

While James, the Lord's brother, is clearly recognized as an apostle (Ac 12:17; 15:13; 21:18; 1 Co 15:7; Ga 1:19; 2:9, 12; Ja 1:1) there is no New Testament reference to how this came about.

e. *Silas, Timothy, etc.*

Silas was simply chosen by Paul and "commended by the brothers" (Ac 15:40).

Timothy, also, was personally chosen by Paul (Ac 16:1-4) - but not, initially, as an apostle. At some point, he was commissioned by prophecy and laying on of hands by a group of elders (1 Ti 1:18; 4:14; 2 Ti 1:6).

About the appointment of other New Testament apostles, we have little or no information.

f. *Summary*

Apart from Matthias, none of the New Testament apostles was actually "appointed" in a technical sense at all. They were either called by God for the task, or "grew" into it by association with existing apostles. Prayer and waiting on God were clearly an accepted part of this process, although not mentioned in every case.

Again we see that the New Testament emphasis is on ministry rather than office. Hence, although Paul, for instance, may call himself an apostle, he is also likely to refer to himself as a "servant" (Ro 1:1; Ph 1:1; Tit 1:1). Timothy is usually labeled a "brother" rather than an apostle (2 Co 1:1; Cl 1:1; 1 Th 3:2; Phm 1, etc.). Peter calls himself an apostle (1 Pe 1:1), but also an "elder" (1 Pe 5:1) and a "servant" (2 Pe 1:1). James describes himself, too, as a "servant" (Ja 1:1).

We do not find the term "apostle" - or "pastor" or "teacher" or anything else, for that matter - being used as a title in the New Testament. Such terms are always descriptions of function and ministry.

The simple position seems to be that such ministry is imparted by God and recognized by man - but never appointed by man.

This would seem to be a wise procedure to follow today.

2.4   Appointment of Elders and Deacons

While the terms "elder" and "pastor" are synonymous and therefore refer to one of the ministry gifts of Ep 4, yet the localized nature of shepherding seems, in one sense, to put it into a different category from the other ministry gifts.

So the New Testament does refer to the actual appointment of elders.

The key text here is Ac 14:23: "*Paul and Barnabas appointed elders for them in each church* (lit. church by church) *and, with prayer and fasting, committed them to the Lord.*"

The word "appointed" here, has been the cause of much debate. Congregationalists claim that it means "to elect by show of hands." Many Episcopalians believe that it means to "ordain by laying on of hands." Presbyterians usually combine both meanings!

The word concerned is *cheirotoneo* - it means literally, "to stretch out the hand." From this, it had the original meaning in New Testament Greek of "to elect by show of hands" and then, simply "to elect" without the method being prescribed. (See Moulton and Milligan, p. 687). In other words, like the English word "elect" it seems possible to use it in a variety of ways, with no special reference to the method of election.

Certainly, in this verse, the subject of the sentence is clearly, "Paul and Barnabas." They appointed the elders. Whether *cheirotoneo* implies that they stretched out their hands to indicate who they wanted, or to lay hands on them, or to ask the people also to raise their hands in a vote, we do not know. Then they prayed, fasted, and committed them to the Lord.

(Note: if the pattern of Ac 13:1 ff is followed, laying on of hands would come after a time of prayer, not before.)

The only other usage of the verb *cheirotoneo* is in 2 Co 8:19, in reference to the brother (Luke?) "chosen" by the churches of Macedonia. Again, the method used is not known.

Titus is told by Paul to "appoint" elders in every city (1:5). The word used here means simply to "set in place." Other than the fact that it was Titus who was to do this, we do not really know how it was done.

Certainly, both Timothy and Titus were told very clearly that no-one should be appointed as an elder who did not meet the conditions of integrity and uprightness that were required.

Paul's reference to the Ephesian elders having been placed by the Holy Spirit (Ac 20:28) reminds us again that whatever human methodology was employed, the Holy Spirit's choice was crucial and fundamental.

The only reference we have to the actual appointing of deacons is possibly Ac 6:1-7. The procedure here was:

-a recommendation from the apostles

-nominations by the church

-prayer and laying on of hands by the apostles

Again, we do not really know how the nominations were carried out.

There is one piece of additional information in Paul's letter to Timothy. Here, we see that, as with elders, deacons were not to be appointed unless they fulfilled certain character and personal qualifications (1 Ti 3:8-12). Furthermore, they were to be thoroughly tested - which may possibly mean being put on probation for a time - before being allowed to serve as deacons (3:10).

From Acts 15, however, we see an early church decision-making process in action. Basically, it took the following form;

>-the apostles and elders meet for discussion (vs. 6)

>-various viewpoints are expressed (vs. 7-21)

>-the apostles and elders, with the whole church, reach a decision (vs. 22)

>-they believe that their decision seems "good" both to them and to the Holy Spirit (vs. 28).

The process here would seem to be that the initiative comes from the leaders, but that the church is invited to approve (or otherwise?) the decision.

In his first letter to the Corinthians (AD 96), Clement seems to see a similar procedure for the appointment of elders. He writes:

>"Similarly, our apostles knew, through our Lord Jesus Christ, that there would be dissensions over the title of bishop. In their full foreknowledge of this, therefore, they proceeded to appoint the ministers I spoke of, and they went on to add an instruction that if these should fall asleep, other accredited persons should succeed them in their office. In view of this, we cannot think it right for these men now to be ejected from their ministry, when, after being commissioned by the apostles (or other reputable persons at a later date) with the full consent of the church, they have since been serving Christ's flock in a humble, peaceable and disinterested way ..." (Par. 44).

Finally, Calvin presents a similar position. He says:

>"Paul and Barnabas selected two, but the whole body, as was the custom by Greeks in election, declared by show of hands, which of the two they wised to have ... Rightly does Cyprian contend for it as the divine authority, that the priest be chosen in the presence of the people, before the eyes of all, and be approved as worthy and fit by public judgment and testimony...

>"We see then that ministers are legitimately called according to the Word of God when those who may have seemed fit are elected on the consent and approbation of the people. Pastors, however, ought to preside over the election, lest any error should

be committed by the general body either through levity, passion, or tumult." (*Institutes*, IV, 3, 15).

Thus Calvin sees that the right of appointment rests in the hands of the existing ministry, but that the people should be given the opportunity to endorse the appointment.

3. SUMMARY

In New Testament days, ministry was imparted by God and then recognized by man.

When human organization, or laws of the state, require specific methodology for appointment, the approach taken should be the one most acceptable and practical in the circumstances. The New Testament does not give specific details about this.

What procedure should be adopted for nomination, voting, election, appointment, etc., must be decided by the people concerned.

The fundamental issue, however, must not be overlooked: that God alone can make a ministry; the best that man can do is to recognize it!

Such recognition should ultimately take the form of prayer, normally with the laying on of hands, and a commissioning by the church to the task in hand.

LESSON SEVEN

THE FAMILY OF GOD

INTRODUCTION

During 1979, the denomination to which I belong was experiencing considerable debate over the question of organization and structure. As I had to chair a conference on this subject, I was deeply concerned to find some biblical and yet practical proposal that would help us to find some answers.

Searching for some point of reference, I asked myself, "What is there in the secular world that provides the best model for comparison with the church? Democracy? Monarchy? Dictatorship? Socialism? Trade Unions? The Army? The Navy? Service Clubs?

I realized instantly that there is one institution that is basic to all human society, has endured from the beginning of time, is, like the church, divinely ordained and is built on *life* as well as *law*.

That institution is, of course, the *family*.

This realization was like a revelation! Immediately, I saw that if the church is to flourish, it must do so on family principles. Just as the family has survived all kinds of pressures, so will the church.

Further, this analogy is thoroughly biblical, for God himself talks of the church as a family (1 Ti 3:15; Ga 6:10; etc.).

In a matter of an hour or two, a panorama of similarities opened up to me, which I later presented to the conference.

The concept seemed to be a word of wisdom for the occasion, and it was received with grace.

The following section is an expanded version of the original presentation -

(I) A LOVING FAMILY

1.   BACKGROUND

The word "family" as such does not occur in the Greek New Testament. Probably "household" is a better translation.

Etymology:

> *oikos* - house. Used of both the building (e.g. Lu 1:23; Ac 2:2) or the people who live in it (Mt 10:6; Lu 11:7; Ac 16:31 etc.).
>
> Occurs 110 times in the New Testament.
>
> *oikeios* - member of a household: used in the plural with the meaning of "family."
>
> Occurs only 3 times in the New Testament.

It is usually obvious whether *oikos* means the *building* or the *people*. The only time it is used in reference to the church (1 Ti 3:15), it clearly means the people. (There were no church buildings at that time, anyway.) Otherwise, the plural *oikeios* is used (Ga 6:10; Ep 2:19).

The family image is, however, frequently implied in places like Ep 4:14 ("*no longer infants*"); the regular use of the term "*brothers*" (Ro 12:1 etc.); references to "*brotherly love*" (Ro 12:10), "*fathers*" in the faith (1 Co 4:15); etc.

It should also be noted that in many cases the New Testament household probably included servants and/or slaves (for example, Philemon's household).

2.   WHAT IS A FAMILY?

The concept of "family" is founded in God (Ep 3:15). The Trinity is actually family - hence, God is totally self-sufficient and self-fellowshipping.

> *   **Think Spot**: *compare the popular idea that God created man because he "needed someone to love." Is this valid?*

The simplest form of human family is the modern nuclear family. This is initially simply husband and wife, but is fully realized when children are born. It may be represented thus:

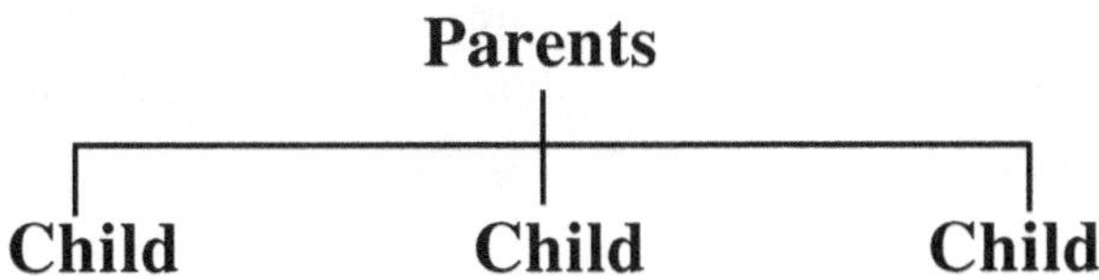

The older, and biblical concept of the family, was the extended family. This may be represented thus:

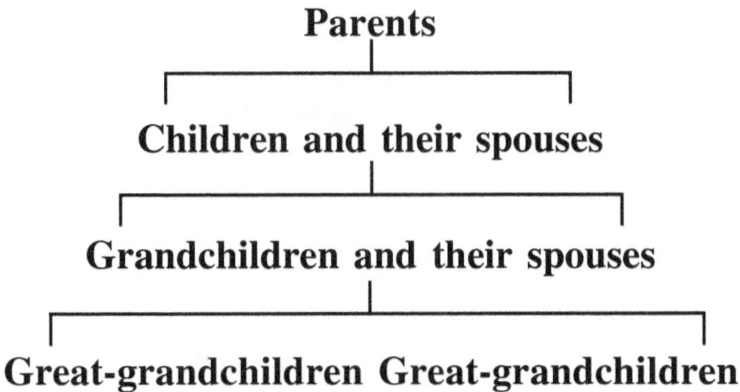

Plus - retainers, servants, and others.

Biblical examples of such families are those of *Adam* (Ge 5:1 ff), *Noah* (Ge 7:1 ff; 10:1 ff), *Abraham* (Ge 14:14; 25:1 ff), *Jacob* (Ex 1:1-5).

So when the Bible speaks of the church as a family, the extended family is the model.

Note: for the sake of simplicity, I will refer only to male members ("fathers," "uncles," "brothers") from this point, with no reference to female members ("mothers," "aunts," "sisters"). This is no reflection on women or women's ministry, but simply a practical choice. I am also using letters of the alphabet to represent both men and churches, which is an over-simplification, but provides a useful and workable model for this study.

3. APOSTLES AND THE CHURCH AS A FAMILY

3.1 THE ROLE OF FATHER

As we have seen, a study of the New Testament shows that the founding of churches was an integral part of apostolic ministry. Hence, an apostle corresponds to the father of a family.

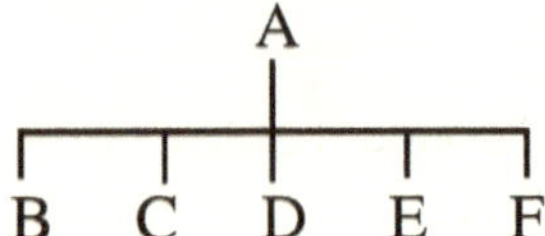

A is the apostle (father) who brings *B-C-D-E-F* to birth.

In New Testament terms, this shows the apostolic authority and care that A has over the churches he has founded. He is not just an "instructor," but a "father" (1 Co 4:15).

Like any father he has:

- authority over the family

- responsibility for the family

The letter to the Galatians clearly shows these two factors.

Research: the letter to the Galatians actually illustrates all aspects of apostolic ministry - authority over a group of churches, apostolic qualifications, supernatural ministry, teaching, instruction, care and concern, etc. Make a list of these points.

3.2 THE ROLE OF "GRANDFATHER"

In any normal family, the sons themselves become fathers in due course. This may be shown thus:

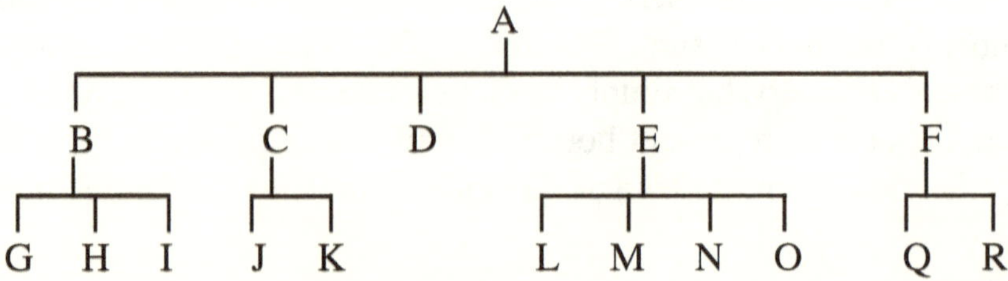

So *A* is now "father" to *B-F* and "grandfather" to *G-R*. Thus, with his "grandchildren" he has:

- *respect*

- and *influence*.

See the letters to the Romans and the Colossians, both assemblies not directly founded by Paul, but as his "grandchildren" showing him respect and accepting his influence.

3.3   THE ROLE OF "SON"

What happens when *A* dies or for some other reason ceases to exercise his ministry? Church history indicates several possibilities:

- disintegration and scattering (e.g. Montanism; and various revival movements);

- organization to maintain unity, with or without the "father."

This is the most common development. It has occurred in almost every revival movement, causing it to become a denomination which must go on regardless. Obvious examples can be found in any of the major denominations.

- development of new "father" ministries.

This seems to be the New Testament answer. The integrating factor in the New Testament was the exercise of apostolic (and other) ministry gifts. So Paul promoted mutual giving and concern (2 Co. 8:1 ff); and traveling ministry or letters brought news and a sense of unity (Cl 4:7-9; 16).

The lamentable absence of apostles is one reason for lack of growth, life, and expansion in churches generally today.

a. Not all "sons" become "fathers" (e.g. *D* has no children) and not all "fathers" have the same size families (cp. *C* and *E*). However, consider the following diagram:

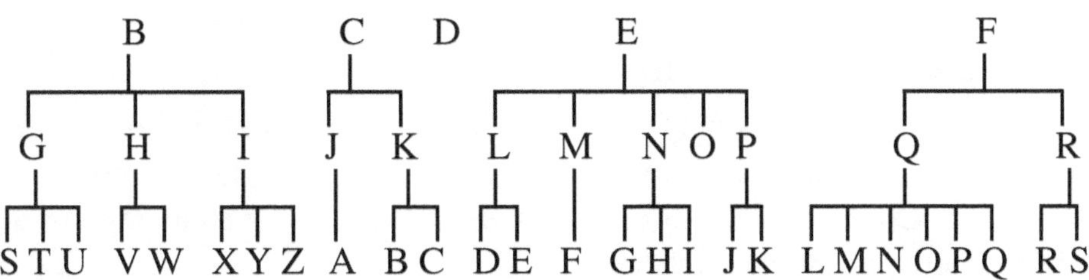

b. *B, C, E* and *F* are the new "fathers." Each has as much responsibility as *A* originally had! It now takes 4 apostles to father the family because the family is so much bigger! To try to replace *A* with one man is to ask him to do more than *A* did - which may well be beyond him - and will certainly stunt growth.

Consider Titus' role as supervisor over a group of churches, even while Paul was alive (Tit 1:5 ff). He was thus exercising a "father" role to churches for which Paul was now "grandfather."

c. Furthermore, *B, C, E* and *F* are now themselves "grandfathers" with influence over, and respect from, *S-S*.

d. Finally, note that if *Y* and *M* "marry," they now have two fathers, *I* and *Q*. This suggests that more than one apostle may have influence over a church or group of churches, and each will be recognized and heeded because of the authority of his ministry.

4. THE PROPHET AND THE CHURCH AS A FAMILY

A prophet may correspond to an "uncle." Consider *D* in the family diagram. He has no children of his own, but just as an uncle may visit, bringing gifts and good things for the family, so a prophet may visit a congregation, bringing inspiration and encouragement, imparting spiritual gifts, and generally blessing the assembly (cp. 1 Co 14:4; Ac 11:27; 15:32).

5. THE EVANGELIST AND THE CHURCH AS A FAMILY

When a child is born, the birth may take place in the home, with the help of a midwife (or her assistant).

Thus in any local church, spiritual children will be born regularly, with the assistance and care of "midwives" in the church.

However, in modern society, we usually have maternity hospitals where specialist facilities are provided to achieve safe and happy childbirth. This corresponds to the ministry of the evangelist who greatly assists in bringing to birth spiritual offspring.

Hence evangelists may visit churches from time to time to assist in bringing to birth those in whom spiritual seed has been planted (compare Ga 4:19; 1 Co 3:5-9), and larger churches may well have an evangelist as a permanent part of the ministry team.

6.   THE PASTOR AND THE CHURCH AS A FAMILY

A pastor corresponds to a "father" or guardian. Like an apostle, a pastor may be a "father" to his people. So his family will grow and perhaps become many families - in which case his ministry develops into that of an apostle. However, it may also be that he himself is not really responsible for the "birth" of the spiritual children in his care. So he becomes a guardian - caring for the children of another (see Ac 20:28; 1 Co 4:15).

> *   **Think Spot**: *Should a pastor whose flock does not grow much necessarily become discouraged?*

7.   THE TEACHER AND THE CHURCH AS A FAMILY

In any family, basic teaching is normally done by the parents - indeed, if family life is to be healthy and if children are to develop well, it must be done by them.

So it is the responsibility of the pastors to provide basic foundational teaching in the church: no-one else can or should do this. (Hence, the close link between pastoral and teaching ministry in Ep 4:11). There is no substitute for the local church.

But it is also normal for children to be sent to school for specialist instruction. This is where the teaching ministry serves the family of God. It can work in either of two ways:

-the teacher comes to the congregation (as a governess might be employed by a large or prosperous family).

-the students go to the teacher (as children go to school). So the disciples gathered themselves to Jesus.

The House of Tabor for example, is attempting to fulfill both these roles by sending teachers and teaching material to churches and by inviting students to assemble where teachers are functioning. [27]

---

[27] Editor's note: *The House of Tabor* is a multi-faceted Christian education center, located in Adelaide, South Australia. Barry Chant is the founder and director of the center. The House of Tabor publishes books and the magazine *New Day International*; it conducts conferences and seminars; it organizes adult education classes on many subjects; and it operates Tabor Bible College.

Paul's home town was Tarsus. The pictures
show a Roman bridge on the road to Tarsus
and the Roman gateway to the city. (Ac. 21:39)

8.   THE FAMILY OF FAITH

We have considered grandfathers, fathers, guardians, servants, in relation to the family of faith.

What about brothers and sisters? This is the final great area of relationships. All that I have said about mutual responsibilities, respect, support, implies brotherly love.

If we *"let brotherly love continue"* (He 13:1) and stand together *"as one man"* (Ph 1:27), each considering others *"better than ourselves"* (2:3), we will see God's family growing and thriving in the world. It will grow and be built up in love (Ep 4:16).

John 13:35 will then be fulfilled.

(II) A WORSHIPING FAMILY

INTRODUCTION

In this section, we shall briefly look at a number of aspects of New Testament church life that are relevant to churches today.

The focus here will be on the more practical side (rather than the doctrinal, which is covered in other DCC courses). What form did New Testament worship take? What order of service was followed, if any? What did it mean to be in "fellowship?" What about the involvement of women? How were the purity, holiness, and teaching of the churches kept unsullied? How were offenders disciplined? What about money? What were the practical aspects of giving?

The N.T. gives a surprising amount of detail on such questions, and much of it is relevant to church practice today.

1. WORSHIP IN THE NEW TESTAMENT CHURCH

There are two aspects of cultural background against which N.T. church worship must be assessed. These are the *Greek Mystery Religions* and the *Jewish Synagogue*.

1.1 MYSTERY RELIGIONS

Mystery cults and religions were popular in Greek-speaking countries in the centuries immediately preceding N.T. days. Because Palestine was highly influenced by Greek culture under Seleucid rule, and because many of the early churches were in Greek colonies, early N.T. worship either reacted against or responded to that common and familiar style. The "mystery" cults took their name from the word *musterion* (which simply means "*anything hidden or secret*"), because only those who passed the initiation tests were admitted to the secret rites of the religion.

These religious practices centered particularly around well known Greek gods such as Dionysius (Bacchus), and they were closely related to seed-time and spring-time (that is, to fertility rites). They were annual (rather than weekly) celebrations which could involve any Greek citizen, male or female, but not slaves, criminals, and enemies.

The initiates (*mustai*) took an oath of secrecy and then underwent the following stages:

> - preliminary purification (by bathing in water)
>
> - rites, sacrifices, and fasts
>
> - the initiation proper (in the temple)
>
> - the last grade of initiation (which was very secret, involving sacred objects)

Eating, drinking, sacrifices, processions, mystic rites, all combined in an impressive array.

It seems clear that Paul's use of the word *musterion* to describe the great divine secret of the gospel, which God had kept hidden for years, was a deliberate attempt to show how much greater was the gospel than the mystery cults (see especially Ep 3:8-12; also Ro 11:28; 16:25-26; Ep 5:32; Cl 1:27; etc.).

In other words, the New Testament church saw its worship more in contrast with than in similarity to the mystery cults. The great divine secret of the gospel was not just for the initiated - it was for all. Furthermore, it was not some paltry, mystic rite in a darkened temple at midnight - it meant a glorious, life-changing encounter with the living God; and one's own body became the temple in which the divine presence is encountered! (Cl 1:27 and 1 Co 6:19-20).

1.2   SYNAGOGUES

Synagogues are frequently mentioned in the New Testament but never in the Old Testament. The origins of the synagogue lie in the inter-testamental period.

Basically, the synagogue was a teaching institution. Some see the beginnings of the synagogue idea in passages describing the Exile, such as Ez 8:1; 20:1-3 (but not in Ps 74:8, where the KJV rendering is misleading).

The synagogue became a place where Mosaic law was taught (cp. Ac 15:21), and where the prophecy of Ezekiel (that after the Return there would be a new spirit and a new heart among the people) was constantly reinforced (Ez 36:26 ff). Certainly, idolatry was never again a problem among the Jews - and the synagogues have been a vital factor in its prevention.

From extra-biblical sources, and from the ruins of synagogues in north Galilee, we learn that those buildings usually lay north-south, with a southern entrance of one main door and two smaller doors. Worshipers usually faced towards Jerusalem, even if it was to the south. The Torah (the law) was kept in a sacred "press." There were various other objects of furniture such as lectern, reading desk, and so on.

Synagogues also served as schools for Jewish boys, possibly with a special room set aside for this purpose.

It should be carefully noted that a synagogue was not a temple. There was neither priest nor sacrifice. It did, however, provide teaching, instruction, and the opportunity for worship for Jewish people wherever they were, and whether or not they could go to the temple.

The New Testament tells us much about synagogue worship. It was characterized by the following:

a. *Corporate activity*

The Greek word sunagoge means *"bringing together."* Synagogues were obviously places where people gathered.

b. *Scripture reading*

Jesus was asked to read from Isaiah (Lu 4:16 ff). Paul preached at Perga after the reading *"from the Law and the Prophets"* (Ac 13:14-15). See also Ac 15:21.

c. *Exposition and teaching*

Jesus frequently taught in synagogues (Mt 9:35; 13:54; Mk 1:21, 39; etc.), as did Paul (Ac 9:20; 13:5; 13:14 ff; 14:1; 17:10; 18:19). Obviously, teaching was a regular part of synagogue worship.

d. *Discussion*

Not only were the scriptures read and taught, but there was also much discussion about them. So Jesus was challenged there about his attitude to the Sabbath (Mt 12:9 ff). Paul spent a great deal of time in synagogues discussing the scriptures (Ac 17;1-4, 17; 18:4, 19; 19:8; 24:12).

e. *Prayer*

People obviously prayed in synagogues (see Mt 6:2, 5) although the temple was seen as the major place of prayer (Lu 18:10; 19:46).

f. *Discipline*

Religious discipline and correction were an accepted role for synagogue officials. So Jesus warned the disciples that they would be flogged there (Mt 10:17; 23:34). Eviction from the Synagogue was a form of punishment (Jn 9:22; 12:42; 16:2). Through the synagogues, Saul of Tarsus intended to apprehend believers (Ac 9:2; 22:19; 26:11).

g. *Trial*

Just as discipline could be administered through a synagogue, so offenders could be "tried" there - hence synagogues had also the function of courts (see Lu 12:11; 21:12).

h. *Privilege and rank*

To have an important position in a synagogue was considered a mark of privilege and rank - usually indicated by having special seats and other favors (Mt 23:6; Mk 12:39; Lu 11:43). Certain men were recognized as "rulers" of the synagogue (Lu 8:41; 13:14) who decided who would read scripture or perform other functions (Ac 13:15).

i. *Ritual*

There were certain accepted rituals. For instance, it seems that men and women were separated and could not sit together (cp. 1 Co 14:34 ff). It was customary to stand to read scripture (Lu 4:16) but not necessarily to teach (cp. Ac 13:16; Lu 4:20 ff).

It is probable that there were prescribed forms of prayer, also (e.g. De 6:4).

The Sabbath day was the normal day of worship (Lu 4:16; Ac 13:14; etc.).

Some synagogues had distinctive emphases and were attended by particular groups of Jews (e.g. Ac 6:9; 17:1-4).

j. *Giving*

Synagogues were also places where gifts could be made for the needy (Mt 6:2-4; whether some actually blew trumpets to announce their gifts may be questioned - Jesus may have been using hyperbole - but obviously it was possible to give publicly and to receive praise for doing so).

A study of the New Testament makes it clear that the worship of the early church was in many respects similar to, and indeed modeled on, synagogue patterns of worship.

1.3   WORSHIP IN THE EARLY CHURCH

Jesus laid down the principle of worship when he said, *"God is Spirit, and his worshipers must worship in spirit and in truth"* (Jn 4:24).

True worship is spiritual; spiritual worship is true. That is, there can be no place for superficial, formalist, or dishonest worship in God's church. Man sees the outward appearance, but God looks on the heart (1 Sa 16:7). Hence worship must be genuine and sincere - this is far more important than the building or place or ritual used.

We can note the following features of New Testament worship:

a. *Location*

Any suitable location could be used. Initially, this meant people's homes (Ac 2:42; 20:7; Ro 16:5; 1 Co 16:19; Cl 4:15; Phm 2). However, early Christians also tried to use both the Temple (Ac 2:46; 3:1) and synagogues (Ac 9:20; 13:5; 13:14 ff; etc.).

b. *Corporate activity*

Like the Jews, early Christians met together as a group (Ac 2:42; 1 Co 11:18a, 33; Ph 1:27 ff). Temple worship was essentially corporate, rather than individualistic, and this concept of congregational praise was carried over into the church. Hence the Christians were urged to assemble together (He 10:25), and each believer was encouraged to participate in some way (1 Co 14:26).

c. *Scripture reading*

The Old Testament was openly studied (Ac 2:42; 6:2-4; 1 Ti 4:13; etc.).

d. *Exposition and Teaching*

The Old Testament was expounded and taught - together with the new teachings of Jesus and the apostles (Ac 2:42; 18:24 ff; 20:7). Teachers were one of Christ's gifts to his church (1 Co 12:28; Ep 4:11).

e. *Prayer*

Prayer was a vital part of early church worship (Ac 2:42; 3:1; 4:23 ff; 6:4; 13:1; 1 Th 5:17; Ep 6:18; 1 Ti 2:1 ff).

f. *Discipline*

While people were not likely to be flogged in a Christian congregation if they committed an offense (as could happen in the synagogue), there was still a standard of discipline (1 Ti 3:4-5; 1 Co 5:1 ff). See below.

g. *Leadership*

While Christian leaders did not aim for the kind of privilege and rank that synagogue leaders sometimes gained, they were clearly recognized and were undoubtedly needed (Ep 4:11 ff; 1 Ti 3:1 ff; He 13:7, 17).

h. *Sacraments*

The twin sacraments of baptism and communion were observed. Baptism was a ceremony of initiation (Ac 2:41; 8:12; Ro 6:3-4; etc.). Communion was a sacramental fellowship meal betokening the death of Christ (1 Co 11:23 ff). These were uniquely Christian in symbolism, although purification by water, and sacramental or memorial feasts (as the Passover), occurred in both the mystery cults and Judaism.

i. *Music*

Singing and making music were an important part of early church worship. Through music people both praised the Lord and taught one another (Ep 5:18 ff; Cl 3:16). There is some evidence that such worship was spontaneous and associated with spiritual inspiration (1 Co 14:14 ff, 26).

j. *Spiritual gifts*

Spiritual gifts such as prophecy, speaking in tongues, healing, etc., were an integral part of New Testament worship (1 Co 12:8 ff; 21:26; 14:1 ff; Ro 15:19; Ja 5:14 ff; see also 1 Ti 1:18; 4:14; 2 Ti 1:6). These gifts were not restricted to leaders only, but were free to all, as led by the Spirit and guided by the leaders (Ro 12:6 ff; 1 Co 14:26; etc.).

k. *Ritual*

The precise forms that services took are unknown to us. We do not know whether men and women sat together or separately (but see 1 Co 14:34 ff); or whether people stood to read or preach; and so on.

The major feature, in fact, was probably freedom and flexibility. While everything was to be done *"decently and in order"* (1 Co 14:40) it was nevertheless possible for anyone to pray, prophesy, etc. (1 Co 11:1 ff; 14:26). There were formal rites such as baptism and communion, together with less formal practices like anointing with oil for healing (Ja 5:14 f); or laying on of hands (1 Ti 4:14: 5:22).

People usually met in homes on Sundays (Ac 20:7; 1 Co 16:2).

1.4   THE SECOND CENTURY CHURCH

The picture we have presented here of New Testament church worship can be clearly seen in the second century church also.

For instance, a provincial Roman governor in Bithynia, named Pliny, sent a detailed report to the Emperor Trajan, dated c. 112 AD, in which he described early Christian worship and practice and asked what he should do about it. Among other things he says -

> " ... it was their habit on a fixed day to assemble before daylight and recite by turns a form of words to Christ as God; and ... they bound themselves with an oath (*Latin: sacramentum*) ... not to commit theft or robbery or adultery, not to break their word, and not to deny a deposit when commanded. After this

was done, their custom was to depart, and to meet again to take food, but ordinary and harmless food ..."

He goes on to mention that these Christians refused to make offerings to the statue of Trajan, or to curse Christ. He also refers to "deaconesses" and to the "contagion" of the Christian "superstition."

Justin Martyr (d. 165) gives a more detailed description of early Christian worship. He describes baptism, communion, Sunday worship, greeting one another with a kiss, and prayers. A "president" gives thanks for the bread and wine "at considerable length" (*Apology* I.61-67).

Tertullian (c. 160-220) gives a similar description. He also mentions free-will monthly offerings *"to feed the poor and to bury them, for boys and girls who lack property and parents, and then for slaves grown old, and shipwrecked mariners and any who may be in mines, islands, or prisons ..."* (*Apology* 39:1-6).

He also mentions the reading of "genuine" writings of the apostles.

The Didache (c. 160) mentions baptism, communion, prayers, fasting, prophecies, Sunday worship, elders and deacons, etc.

It is interesting to note there however, that set forms of thanksgiving for the bread and wine are prescribed which all must repeat - and that only prophets are free *"to give thanks as they please."* Also set days are laid down for fasting, and set forms for baptism.

Thus we see that within one hundred years of the apostolic age, semi-formal modes of worship and liturgy were being developed - a trend which continued over successive years.

The brief flowering of Montanism in Phrygia in the late second century, with its re-emphasis on prophetic gifts and glossolalia, unfortunately had a reverse effect on the church at large. Because of Montanism's excesses in doctrine and practice (such as extreme eschatology and asceticism) the rest of the church tended to retreat into the safety of prescribed liturgy and ritual, where there was no risk of false prophecies or spontaneous, but erroneous, utterances. It was to be many centuries before this trend was reversed.

1.5   SUMMARY

New Testament church worship then, was heavily modeled on synagogue worship, but also flexible, and free to be "led by the Spirit."

1 Co 14:26 seems to be a description of a high level of involvement on the part of all, but with due recognition of local church leaders (elders, deacons) and God-given ministries (apostles, etc.), as we have seen.

2. FELLOWSHIP IN THE NEW TESTAMENT CHURCH

Fellowship is an assumed and integral part of the New Testament church. By definition, a religion that is characterized by "assemblies" meeting together for worship must have a strong emphasis on fellowship.

Etymology:

koinonia =   fellowship, sharing, participation, contribution, communion.

2.1 PARTNERSHIP

The word *koinonia* is actually derived from *koinonos*, which means "partner."

The word is frequently used outside the New Testament to describe such things as marriage partners, parties to business contracts, and fellow-workers. It is used in the New Testament of James and John who were fishermen in partnership (Lu 5:10) and of Titus being Paul's "partner" and "fellow-worker" (2 Co 8:23).

Hence, to be in fellowship with someone means to be in partnership with them - and this implies some sense of mutual responsibility. It is more than just being "friends."

---

* **Think Spot**: *how much local church "fellowship" really reaches the level of such "partnership?"*

2.2 SHARING

The related verb *koinoneo* means basically "to share." According to one writer, "it is always used of active participation, where the result depends on the co- operation of the receiver as well as on the action of the giver" (Brooke, in Moulton & Milligan, pg. 351).

Hence, Paul asks the Christians in Rome to *"share with God's people who are in need"* (Ro 12:13). See also Ga 6:6. The New Testament also tells of sharing -

> *possessions* (Ac 2:44)
>
> *suffering* (Ph 3:10)
>
> *worship* (Ac 2:42)
>
> *faith* (Phm 6)
>
> *blessings* (1 Co 10:16)
>
> *money* (Ro 15:26-27)
>
> *teaching* (Ac 2:42)
>
> *companionship* (Ga 2:9)

Clearly, for the New Testament believer, fellowship was more than just a handshake or a once-a-week smile and "hello." It was an active sharing with any brother or sister who was in need of all that you were or possessed.

---

* **Think Spot**: *Consider the above list in the light of your own life. How would you rate your "fellowship" on a scale of one to five, if five means "excellent?"*

2.3   PAYING THE PRICE

It is obvious that *koinonia* is not cheap. There is a price to pay!

Compare the fellowship we have with God - it cost him the price of his Son (1 Jn 1:3-9). Similarly, we will have to face the cost of fellowship with our brothers and sisters, too (1 Jn 3:16-18).

---

* **Think Spot**: *What are some practical ways in which we may meet the cost of fellowship?*

2.4   THE COMMUNION SERVICE

An understanding of *koinonia* gives us a deeper appreciation of the Lord's Supper. By it, we are brought into fellowship with God - and with one another (1 Co 10:16 ff).

When we break bread together, we are actually committing ourselves to one another in a specific way; we are obligated to follow our "fellowship" through with genuine sharing with one another.

2.5   ANALOGIES OF FELLOWSHIP

The various analogies of the church I have described above all imply a committed relationship -

> *members of the body*
>
> *bricks in a temple*
>
> *members of a family*
>
> *seed in the ground*
>
> *bride and bridegroom.*

Koinonia in all these cases means being closely joined and interdependently aligned with others. There is clearly no place for independent action.

Paul details this concept in Ep 4:12-16, where he refers to at least three of these analogies (body, family, building). The aim is that God's people might find themselves in unity (vs. 13), stability (vs. 14), and effective function (vs. 16). But this is only by working together in love (vs. 16), being willing to be "joined" to other members of the body in a useful, coordinated fashion (vs. 16).

Although he does not use the word *koinonia*, he is talking about it, nevertheless.

2.6   THE PRACTICE OF FELLOWSHIP

The outstanding passage on fellowship is Ph 2:1 ff. If there is any "fellowship of the Spirit" (which could be rendered, incidentally, as simply "fellowship of spirit"), then certain things should follow. First, believers should (vs. 2):

> *- think the same thing*
>
> *- have the same love*
>
> *- be "fellow-souled"*
>
> *- think the one thing.*

Note the emphasis on thinking here. Effective fellowship depends on right thinking - thinking unity, love, sympathy, purpose, vision.

Disunity and broken fellowship always begin in the mind - without exception. So, in the same way, unity and true fellowship begin there too.

> * **Think Spot**: *Can you think of people now about whom you could think more positively and lovingly?*

Second, Paul declares that true fellowship of spirit means that no-one acts from selfishness, vanity, or conceit (vs. 3). In fact, quite the reverse; each considers others better than himself (vs. 3) - an attitude that can only arise from humility.

Clearly, another major cause of disunity is selfish pride. There can never be real fellowship among the selfish and the proud!

True fellowship demands humility.

> * **Think Spot**: *Can you think of situations right now where your pride is a hindrance to fellowship? What can you do about it?*

Thirdly, true fellowship exists when people are at least as interested in the affairs of others as they are in their own affairs (vs. 4). By contrast, a major hindrance to fellowship is self-pity and/or the desire for sympathy. People who are mostly concerned about their own hurts and needs cannot commit themselves to true fellowship. Koinonia demands a genuine interest in the affairs of others.

The supreme illustration of this is the self-denial, humility, and love of Christ - who gave his all to achieve *koinonia* between God and man (vs. 5:11).

> * **Think Spot**: *Has preoccupation with your self and your own affairs been a hindrance to your fellowship with others?*

2.7   CONCLUSION

A church patterned after the New Testament is marked by genuine *koinonia*. Where there is a deficiency in the latter, there will be serious weakness in the former.

Our attitude should be the same as that of Christ Jesus: who, being in very nature God, did not consider equality with God something to be grasped, but made himself nothing, taking the very nature of a servant, being made in human likeness. And being found in appearance as a man, he humbled himself and became obedient to death - even death on a cross!

Lesson Eight

Making the Church Strong

This lesson continues on from the previous one -

3. Discipline in the New Testament Church

Any effective organization must have some means of disciplining its members. This is true also of the church.

3.1 The Nature of Discipline

First of all, the church is a voluntary organization. Hence, there is really only one form of discipline it can adopt: exclusion from some or all of its privileges. Any attempt to go beyond this, is to do more than is allowed by scripture, or by human right.

Hence, in the New Testament, we read of ultimate discipline taking the form of dis-fellowshipping of the offender. So Jesus taught that one who refused to accept admonition from the whole church should be treated *"as a pagan or a tax-collector"* (Mt 18:17).

> * **Think Spot**: *How should a tax collector or pagan be treated? See Mt 5:43 ff.*

So also, when a member of the Corinthian church committed a gross sexual offense, he was cut off from fellowship (1 Co 5:5, 11).

Where the person in need of discipline is in receipt of some benefit or privilege from the church, this may be withheld as a less severe form of punishment - so a salaried minister may be taken off the payroll without being cut off from fellowship; or a voluntary worker may be removed from office, and so on.

In summary, New Testament discipline is simply the withholding of privilege.

Some of the major abuses of the medieval church lay in the setting up of church courts and the administration of other forms of punishment. The scandal of the Inquisition is well-known. But apart from that, heretics were condemned by the church for no crime other than heresy, and then sentenced to torture or to death. (The church itself did not actually administer the penalty. In order to keep to its role as a "spiritual" body, the church handed the condemned to the secular arm for punishment. So the church pronounced sentence and the state carried it out, such as the burning at the stake of Huss, Cranmer, Latimer, Ridley). Even Calvin was responsible for the burning of Michael Servetus (Oct. 27th 1554) for blasphemy; and both Catholics and Protestants approved the death of people like the Anabaptists.

Such happenings would be impossible in most (if not all) parts of today's church. Nevertheless, churches still need to be careful to avoid going beyond the biblical mandate for discipline.

3.2 THE SCOPE OF DISCIPLINE

There are only two areas in which church discipline may be applied. These are the areas of holiness and truth.

a. *Holiness*

The need for holiness is clearly expressed in scripture, e.g. 1 Pe 1:15-16; 1 Co 6:11-20; Ep 4:17ff; 5:3; He 12:11; etc.

The church must be wary lest any element of evil corrupt the whole (1 Co 5:6-8).

So, in the New Testament, the following sins are disciplined -

> *broken fellowship* (Mt 18:15-17)
>
> *disorderly conduct* (2 Th 3:11 ff)
>
> *laziness* (2 Th 3:6-15)
>
> *divisiveness* (Ro 16:17-18; Tit 3:9-10)
>
> *sexual immorality* (1 Co 5:1-13)
>
> *greed* (1 Co 5:11)
>
> *idolatry* (1 Co 5:11)
>
> *slander* (1 Co 5:11)
>
> *drunkenness* (1 Co 5:11)
>
> *dishonesty* (1 Co 5:11)

Since no exhaustive list of such offenses is given in any one New Testament passage, we may take this list as representative of the kinds of sin that may come under disciplinary action.

b. *Truth*

Salvation means coming to the knowledge of truth (1 Ti 2:4; 2 Ti 3:7; Jn 14:6). To depart from the truth is to depart from God (2 Ti 3:8; 4:2ff; Ga 1:6ff; 2:5; 5:7; etc.).

So those who either depart from the truth or teach others to do so must come under the admonition and/or discipline of the church.

So Paul disciplines Hymenaeus and Alexander for blasphemy (1 Ti 1:20). He speaks angrily of the Judaizers who were bothering and misleading the Galatians (Ga 1:6 ff). John instructs believers neither to fellowship nor bless those who do not hold the teaching of Christ (2 Jn 10-11). And the Lord himself rebukes the church at Pergamum for its failure to deal with the Balaamic and Nicolaitan heresies (Re 2:14 ff).

The only areas of a believer's personal life in which the church may exercise authority are these two. In every other area (home life, employment, relationships, recreation, etc.) the church has no authority - unless there are unscriptural and/or immoral aspects to those activities. Thus believers may choose whatever vocations they desire, without having to be subject to their local oversight or congregation - unless there is some dishonest or immoral practice involved in the job; in which case, the church has the right to speak, to advise, and to admonish.

3.3   THE PURPOSE OF DISCIPLINE

It should also be carefully noted that the purpose of discipline is not to make the church either sinless or free from error.

Those qualities are to be achieved by prayer, faith, study of scripture, the power of the Spirit, fellowship and the like - the whole New Testament makes this abundantly clear (e.g. Ro 8:13; 2 Co 2:14; Ep 2:1 ff; etc.).

The purpose of New Testament discipline is twofold:

a. *The individual*

First, to guide, correct, and restore those who have deliberately and knowingly failed to arrive at either holiness or truth and who persist in their erroneous ways.

Hence, those who exercise discipline should do so in -

> *gentleness* (2 Co 2:4)
>
> *humility* (Ga 6:1)
>
> *prayer* (Mt 18:19-20)
>
> *grace* (2 Co 2:7; 7:10-13).

And the aim of the discipline will be to restore and save the individual concerned. So Jesus spoke of gaining the offending brother (Mt 18:15). Paul saw the salvation of the sinner's spirit as the ultimate goal (1 Co 5:5) - and that he might learn not to sin anymore (1 Ti 1:20). Hence, he wrote a second time to the Corinthians, to express his concern that the offending brother might not be *"overwhelmed by excessive sorrow"* (2 Co 2:7) - and that he should be restored.

The purpose, then, is patterned on the purpose for God's discipline of us as his children - that we might learn afterwards to produce *"a harvest of righteousness and peace"* and that the lame might no longer stumble, but again walk upright (He 12:12).

It would seem that any form of discipline that makes it impossible for the offender to be restored is going beyond the New Testament mandate.

---

*   **Think Spot**: *Someone has said, "The Christian army is the only one that shoots its own wounded." What do you think of this?*

---

b. *The assembly*

The exercise of discipline is also beneficial to the church. The reason for public rebuke (where necessary - see next section) is only that others may be warned (1 Ti 5:20) and thus avoid the same mistake.

Further, Paul goes to some length to explain to the Corinthians that there are two major reasons for the required action. *First*, tolerated sin would affect the whole church, just as yeast affects a whole batch of dough (1 Co 5:6-8). If nothing were done, the whole church would drop its standards and become immoral.

Second, their willingness to discipline was also an expression of their obedience. Although his instructions to them caused them sorrow, it was necessary for their sakes, as well as for the man concerned, that the discipline be applied - for they, too, needed to repent of their attitude towards the sin and act accordingly (2 Co 7:8 ff). So Paul rejoices that their sorrow was a *"godly sorrow"* that produced repentance (vs. 10). And Paul's writing to them was so that they would discover their own real devotion to God (vs. 12).

Thus, disciplinary action and firm setting of standards is beneficial to the assembly as well.

3.4 THE PRACTICE OF DISCIPLINE

Jesus gives us a clear pattern of how to treat an offending brother. If this pattern were observed more often, we would see far fewer problems in our churches and far more people! According to Mt 18:15-18, the following action should be taken:

a. *Personal admonition* (vs. 15)

A personal approach should be made first of all to the offending brother. The issue should be raised honestly and openly, but, as we have seen, with humility and gentleness (Ga 6:1).

The purpose is to gain the brother concerned and to restore fellowship. (It may be that you are in error, and that the brother concerned is actually innocent; in which case this personal meeting will sort this out and clear the air.)

b. *Before witnesses* (vs. 16)

If the first step fails, then two or three witnesses should be called. Here, Jesus simply adopts an Old Testament principle, that at least two witnesses were needed before anyone could be convicted of a crime (De 19:15). Paul makes a similar point about accusations directed at elders - they must be ignored unless made before witnesses (1 Ti 5:19).

So with a problem of fellowship or spiritual offense, witnesses are needed to establish the matter. (Although Jesus does not mention it, it may well be that the witnesses support the "accused" - in which case their judgment must be accepted and fellowship restored with apology and forgiveness all round - and perhaps recognition of misunderstanding.)

To this point, only a small group of people is involved, and if the matter is here resolved, no permanent harm has been done to the standing and acceptance of anyone concerned. Remember, that since the aim of disciplinary action is restoration, it is far better to handle it as quietly as possible so that restoration can be achieved with minimal distress.

Clearly, the witnesses concerned in such a case must be people of integrity who will not have any cause to favor one side or the other. They will normally be the leaders of an assembly.

c. *Before the church* (vs. 17)

Only as a last resort should the matter be brought before the assembly. And then, if the assembly endorses the charges already made, the offender must hear its opinion and abide by it. If he refuses he is to be cut off from fellowship.

Paul makes the same judgment on the Corinthian believer who was guilty of incest (1 Co 5:1 ff).

It is clear that this man was willfully persisting in his sin (vs. 1) and that the church had done nothing about it. So they are told to exercise disciplinary action and to "*hand him over to Satan*" (vs. 5) that is, to cut him off from fellowship and thus leave him in the realm of the god of this world. They are to have no further fellowship with him (vs. 11). See also 1 Ti 1:20. Paul also declares that those who persist in sin are to be openly rebuked before all (1 Ti 5:20).

Note, however, some qualifications to this.

First, it is not always practicable to involve everybody in a church in such matters. For example, in a large congregation a representative group would probably suffice.

Second, when new Christians are involved in such difficult matters as disciplinary action, they may be asked to bear a burden they are not yet ready to bear.

Again a selected group of mature people may be more advisable.

Third, there are some who take 1 Ti 5:20 as applying to "*all the elders*" rather than all the members. This would probably apply in the case of a pastor who sinned, for instance. He would be approached first by a concerned brother, then by two or three brother ministers. If this failed, the matter would be dealt with by an assembly of his fellow pastors - who could come from many churches. In this way, the matter would be handled by a body mature enough to cope with it.

Thus, the matter would not need to be made known to all the members of that church.

(Note that the words recorded in Mt 18:15 ff were spoken before the establishment of the church as such - so we can take the word *ekklesia* in the more general sense of "assembly.")

Fourth, although Jesus says that an offending person should be cut off from fellowship, he is still to be treated *"as a tax collector or pagan"* - so he should still be loved and treated with kindness (cp. 2 Co 2:11). The disciplined person should not be left without hope.

If this pattern of discipline were followed regularly, then many fellowship difficulties would be resolved and churches would be happier and healthier.

> * **Think Spot**: *Consider Mt. 18:15-20 in the light of personal relationships as well; not as a matter of discipline, but simply of dealing with personal problems between fellow-believers.*

It is clear from the above that discipline is not a "sudden-death" matter. Ample opportunity must be given for the offender to repent and be restored. At least two warnings must be given (Tit 3:10) before action is taken. And even then, after cutting someone off from fellowship, every attempt should be made to restore him again.

Note: The word "church" in this section normally applies to the local church - discipline of a local church member must be dealt with by that local church. So Paul tells the Corinthians what to do, but it is they who must do it (1 Co 5:12-13). However, in the case of a minister who fails, this may be best dealt with by an assembly of his fellow ministers.

4.   THE MINISTRY OF WOMEN

To what extent should women be involved in ministry? For some people, that is a highly controversial matter! One of the problems is that we tend to view such an issue from our own cultural perspective.

Hence, to people of our "liberated" generation, New Testament teaching may seem somewhat restrictive. To people of earlier generations, however, New Testament teaching was itself "liberated." Essentially, the biblical picture of the role of women is sound, realistic, and generous.

In examining this subject we shall go to the creational order to see what God's original purpose for woman was. Then we shall see two basic facts. First, that both man and woman stand equal before God. Second, that there are distinct differences. The physical and biological differences are obvious. There are also emotional and spiritual differences. Hence, while there are many things that both men and women can do, certain areas are specifically designated for each.

The following is a brief summary of a complex subject:

4.1   WOMEN'S ROLE IN THE OLD TESTAMENT

Without attempting an exhaustive survey of the Old Testament teaching and practice, it is interesting to note that there were several Old Testament women who occupied positions of leadership and ministry -

Miriam -	a recognized leader among the women, she was strong enough to challenge Moses' leadership (Nu 12:1 ff).
Deborah -	a married woman who was the leader ("judge") of Israel (Jg 4:4).
Noadiah -	a prophetess (Ne 6:14).
Jael -	whom God used to bring down Sisera (Jg 4:9 ff).
Huldah -	a married woman who was recognized as a prophetess (2 Kg 22:14; 2 Ch 34:22).
Athaliah -	who, although wicked, ruled as regent over Israel (2 Kg 11:1-3).
A *"wise woman"* -	whose decision saved many lives (2 Sa 20:14-22).
The *ideal wife* -	whose description depicts a woman of enterprise, business expertise, etc. (Pr 31:10 ff).
Annah -	another prophetess (Lu 2:36-38).

Then there is also the promise of Joel that the Spirit will be poured out on *"both men and women"* (Jl 2:29).

One must add that while women's leadership in Old Testament days was clearly the exception, rather than the rule, it was certainly possible and acceptable.

4.2   NEW TESTAMENT REFERENCES TO WOMEN IN MINISTRY

There are many New Testament references to women undertaking leadership ministry roles. Consider the following:

Mary -	the mother of Jesus, who was among those present before and at Pentecost (Ac 1:14; 2:1-4).
Phoebe -	who was a deacon, and who apparently delivered Paul's letter to the Romans (Ro 16:1-2, 12-13).
Priscilla -	who, together with her husband, was Paul's fellow-worker (Ac 18:2, 18; Ro 16:3), a teacher (Ac 18:26) and a leader of a local church (Ro 16:3-5 1 Co 16:19).
Junia -	who was "outstanding among the apostles" (Ro 16:7).
Tryphena -	another of Paul's fellow-workers (Ro 16:12).
Tryphosa -	another fellow-worker (Ro 16:12).
Persis -	another "worker" (Ro 16:12).
Euodia -	another fellow-worker (Ph 4:2-3).
Syntyche -	another fellow-worker (Ph 4:2-3).
Philip's daughters -	who had recognized prophetic gifts (Ac 21:9).

Then there are general references to women praying and prophesying (1 Co 11:1-16; 1 Ti 2:8-15); to older women teaching the younger (Tit 2:3-4); and to the fact that in Christ both male and female are equal (Ga 3:27-28).

4.3 AREAS OF NEW TESTAMENT MINISTRY OPEN TO WOMEN

The following areas of ministry are clearly open to women in the New Testament:

prophecy -	Ac 2:17-18; 21:9; 1 Co 11:5; 14:31.
evangelism -	Ac 8:1-4; Ro 16:7; Ph 4:3.
teaching -	Ac 18:26; Tit 2:3-4.
prayer -	1 Co 11:5; Ac 16:13 ff.
pastoral ministry -	Ro 16:3-5; 1 Co 16:19.
serving -	as a deacon; Ro 16:1-2; 1 Ti 3:11 (taking "women" here as "women deacons," not "wives of deacons")

apostolic ministry -	possibly implied by the references to Junia (Ro 16:7), Priscilla (16:3; 1 Co 16:19) and Euodia and Syntyche (Ph 4:2-3).
spiritual gifts -	there is nothing in the key passages on this subject (Ro 12:3 ff; 1 Co 12:7 ff) to suggest that such gifts were restricted only to men. Indeed, on the basis of Jl 2:28 ff and Ac 2:17 ff, together with Ac 1:14 and 2:1-4, we may well believe exactly the opposite.

4.4   RESTRICTIONS ON WOMEN'S MINISTRY

To balance the points made in the previous two sections, however, it should be pointed out that there are also restrictions on women's ministry given in the New Testament.

The major restriction seems to be in the area of authority. In simple terms, a woman may do all that a man may do, except take leadership.

Consider the following:

a. *Creational order*

A woman's role is to assist a man (Ge 2:18). This does not mean servility - she is his companion as well as his helper. (Note, too, that the word *"helper"* used here, occurs 21 times in the Old Testament, 15 in reference to God being the helper of men!) But it does clearly express the leadership role that God assigned to man.

Paul appeals to this creational order, too, when he says that *"Adam was formed first, then Eve"* (1 Ti 2:13). Hence, he does not permit a woman to *"teach"* or *"exercise authority"* over a man (1 Ti 2:12).

A woman may teach, of course, but Paul apparently required her to do so either together with her husband (e.g. Priscilla and Aquila - Ac 18:26; Ro 16:3-5, etc.), or with other women (Tit 2:4).

The word translated "to have authority" (*authentein*) has connotations of independence. It can be translated as *"to domineer over"* (Souter) or *"to act on one's own authority"* (ENT).

When Eve acted in this way and *"taught"* Adam, she led him into error (v. 14). Her attempt to lead and teach, in defiance of the creational order, led to disaster.

Elsewhere in the N.T., the husband is spoken of as the "*head*" of the wife (Ep 5:23) and the man as the "*head*" of the woman (1 Co 11:3-4; note that the same Greek words can be translated respectively both "man" and "husband," and "woman" or "wife." The context determines the choice of English word.) Although there has been much debate about the meaning of the word "*head*," it has several obvious meanings. These include -

> leadership
>
> guidance
>
> direction

Some degree of authority is implied as well, as the leadership of a man over a woman is compared with the headship of Christ over a man (1 Co 11:3; Ep 5:23). In the same way, God is head over Christ (1 Co 11:3).

> * **Think Spot**: *Does this mean that Christ is less than God as regards his Person? In the light of this, compare 1 Co 11:3 with Ga 3:28.*

The word "head" therefore implies a difference in role but not in worth or status. Nor does it imply dominance by the man and degrading submission by the woman. As Paul points out elsewhere, in Christ, male and female are one (Ga 3:28). Their standing is equal. However, this has no bearing on differences in role, function and ministry. There are certain differences between men and women!

The creational plan was for man to lead, but for woman to give him able assistance in every possible way.

Although a full discussion of Ep 5:21 ff, is not relevant here, it is interesting to note that both husband and wife are to submit to each other - as indeed all believers are to do (vs. 21). Further, the husband is to be both the lover (vs. 25) and savior of his wife (vs. 23), as well as the head.

One might make the same points about a pastor/elder. He can only be leader if he also loves and "saves" his people, and submits to them - including the women!

b. *Argument from silence*

What the N.T. does not say here may be as important as what it does say. Although argument from silence can be dangerous, it may in this case be significant. For instance -

Jesus placed no women among the Twelve. There were, of course, women who followed him loyally and faithfully (Mt 27:55; Lu 23:27; 23:49, 55-56). But they were never numbered among the disciples. Their role was essentially a "helping" one (Lu 8:2-3). The women whom Paul calls "fellow-workers" possibly exercised a similar role.

Furthermore, there are no N.T. references to women elders: that is, leadership in a local church is nowhere exercised by a woman. The nearest we come to this is Priscilla - it is clear that she was joint leader with her husband of the church in their house (Ro 16:3-5; 1 Co 16:19). Priscilla evidently had a fairly dominant role - her name is mentioned before Aquila's in 3 of the 5 N.T. references to them - nevertheless, she was not the sole leader.

However, such muting of the feminine role in the early church may be more a bowing to cultural pressure than an expression of God's eternal purpose.

4.5   DIFFICULT PASSAGES

a. *1 Co 11:1-22*

The reference appears to be to customs with which we are no longer familiar - e.g. of veiling the face, or at least the brow. A detailed analysis is not necessary here, but the following points can be made:

> - man is the head of woman, as Christ is of man and God of Christ (vs. 3).

> - a woman may both pray and prophesy publicly (prophecy is by definition public) (vs. 4-5).

> - a man should pray with his head uncovered; a woman with her head covered (vs. 4-6).

> - the reason for this is that man was created first in God's image, while woman was created for man. The covering of the head is a sign of this (vs. 7-10).

> - since angels are witnesses of Christian worship, such order ought to be observed (vs. 10; cp. 1 Co 4:9; Ac 1:10; He 1:14; 12:22; etc.).

- a woman's long hair is an indication of her need for covering (vs. 13-16).

- nevertheless, both man and woman are equal before God; for as woman was created for man, so man is born of woman. Neither is independent of the other (vs. 11-12).

The main sense of the passage is this:

- man has a leadership role;

- but woman is in no way inferior to man.

Note: does this passage mean that women today should always have their heads covered when they pray, preach, or prophesy? Opinions are divided about that.

First, some aspects of the passage are not clear; e.g. what does Paul really mean in vs. 10, "*because of the angels,*" and "*authority on her head?*" (Barnes, on his page 5, is honest: "I confess ... I do not know what it means)."

Second, there are cultural factors not so relevant today. From that day to this, it has been customary for Jewish men to pray with heads covered; but both Roman men and women prayed with heads *uncovered*. Shaving of the head was an accepted punishment for adulteresses and a frequent sign of slavery. Corinthian prostitutes tended to walk the streets unveiled (ENT. II 872).

Further, heathen priestesses were wont to utter their oracles in frenzied fashion with hair untidy and uncovered (Barnes, pg. 754).

On the other hand, for a man to remove his hat in the presence of a superior was and is still a mark of respect.

In the light of all this, it appears that Paul was trying to establish a distinctive Christian pattern that would be consistent with the order of creation.

Given the fact that this is the only N.T. passage on this concept, and given the uncertainty that surrounds it, many Christian women today feel that head covering is not mandatory in contemporary public worship, It must be a matter of individual conscience.

The major point of the passage is, however, quite clear, as we have seen above.

> b. *1 Co. 14:34-36*

This passage appears to prohibit women from speaking in the assembly altogether. However, as we have seen, there is plenty of N.T. evidence of women prophesying, praying, worshipping, evangelizing, and teaching.

Possibly, the men and women at Corinth sat in separate sections of the meeting place (cp. the synagogue), in which case, for women to ask questions of their husbands may well have been disruptive.

Another interesting possibility is that in verses 34-35 Paul is actually quoting something that the Corinthian men were saying - that it was they who refused permission to their women to speak, and that Paul clearly refutes this in verses 36-37. (See J. Sidlow-Baxter, vol. 5, pg. 114 f).

Hence, we actually have here an approval for women to express themselves publicly in services of worship!

4.6 SUMMARY

There is abundant N.T. evidence for active ministry by women in the church. The main exception may lie in the area of recognized leadership and authority. Some commentators feel that scripture prohibits women from serving in those capacities; hence they resist the idea of women pastors and elders, or of women being ordained as priests, and the like. Other commentators feel that the restraints on women holding high office in the church were based on cultural and social custom rather than on inviolable spiritual principle. Since those customs have lost their force in modern society, and it is no longer offensive to the community for a women to be given authority, it is argued that the biblical restraints are no longer mandatory.

Those who adopt the latter view believe that the primary idea behind the biblical injunctions against a woman *"teaching"* or *"having authority over men,"* is not the place of woman in society, but rather the need for the church to avoid hindering the gospel by unnecessarily offending contemporary mores. In Paul's day that principle required the exclusion of women from high office in the church; *in our day the same principle might require the exact opposite ruling* - in other words, the modern church will cause needless offense if it excludes women from high office.

Those who adopt the former view believe that Paul's use of the primeval order of creation to enforce his apparent ruling against a woman *"teaching or exercising authority"* (1 Ti 2:11-14) shows that he was indeed dealing with an unchanging spiritual law, which taught that women must maintain a subordinate role. Such a law (they say) is not affected by social conditions, hence it is still spiritually wrong, as it was in Paul's day, for a woman to be given the office of pastor, elder, priest.

However that argument may be resolved, it remains clear that women were very active in the N.T. church, at all levels of ministry (if not authority), and that the modern church would do well to copy that paradigm and to use as widely as possible the special gifts and abilities of those women God has called into the body of Christ.

Lesson Nine

Oblation and Sacrament

Your previous lessons began an exploration of the church as a worshipping community. We have looked at the fellowship and discipline that functions in the church, and at the place of women in its ministry. This lesson continues that exploration. Our theme is the place of oblation and sacrament in the church. We begin with *oblation*, that is, the concept of Christian giving.

Giving is an important part of church worship and fellowship. In both Old and New Testaments, the bringing of one's material possessions to God is given strong emphasis.

1. Oblation

1.1 The Basis for Giving

Essentially, all giving is a natural response of gratitude to God. So Abraham (Ge 14:20) and Jacob (Ge 28:22) spontaneously gave a tenth of their produce to the Lord. Similarly, Zacchaeus spontaneously gave to the poor after his encounter with Jesus (Lu 19:8).

Old Testament writers saw everything as being God's in the first place (Ps 24:2; 50:10; Hg 2:8). Hence, all giving and tithing is a symbolic and representative acknowledgment of this. The result of so "honoring" the Lord will be increased prosperity and bountiful harvest (Pr 3:9-10). Indeed giving is itself like planting seed. Only as a man "scatters" what he has will it return to him again: what he withholds, he loses (Pr 11:24-25).

The N.T., too, points out that all things are God's in the first place and that giving is simply the act of a good steward, faithfully returning to his master what is rightly his (1 Co 3:21-23; 4:1-2; 2 Co 8:6 ff).

1.2 Tithing

The basis of O.T. giving was the tithe - i.e. one tenth of one's income. Concerning tithing, we note the following:

a. *Before the Law*

It is often assumed that tithing was first inaugurated as part of the law of Moses. In fact, the practice of tithing goes back at least to the time of Abraham, who tithed the spoils of war to Melchizedek (Ge 14:22; He 7:2, 6); and also to Jacob, who offered to give back to God a tenth of all that God gave him (Ge 28:22) - which indicates an habitual and regular pattern of living.

b. *Under the Law*

By the time of Moses, tithing had become a clearly established pattern and it was included in the Mosaic Laws.

There are some difficulties in reconciling the various passages on the subject, as two different purposes for the tithe seem to be given.

(i) First of all, according to Nu 18:21ff, all tithes were to be directed to the Levites, who were given no actual inheritance in the land of Canaan, the Lord himself being their inheritance (vs. 23-24). They were also given possession of 48 towns, so that they could care for their families and flocks (Nu 35:1-8; Js 21:1 ff), but no actual tribal territory. This was possibly to prevent the priestly class from becoming too well entrenched and hence too powerful (cp. Ge 47:22).

Every Israelite was expected to give one tenth of all produce (i.e. grain and fruit) and the tenth animal born to his flock each year to the Lord (Le 27:30-33). If he wished, he could give the tithe in money rather than kind, but in this case, he had to add one fifth to its value (Le 27:31).

Furthermore, he had to select the tenth animal simply as it came in the tally, whether it was good or bad (Le 27:32). If he was found attempting a "swap," both animals were to be given to the Lord (Le 27:33).

The principal here is clear - the tithe was to be given regardless of inconvenience or difficulty or personal circumstances.

The Levites, in turn, could use the tithes as a source of food, and were free to provide for their families in this way (Nu 18:31-32).

However, they in turn were expected to tithe to the high priest and his family (Nu 18:25-28). Moreover, it was not to be just a tenth, but the best tenth; that is, the finest of grain, stock, etc., that they had themselves received (Nu 18:29).

(The high priest also received all the meat and grain offerings presented at the altar, except for the choice portions, and except for the burnt offerings - Nu 18:8-11; Le 7:28-36; Le 6:8-13; 1:9. Furthermore, the first fruits of each crop and the first born of each flock were also given to the high priest - Nu 18:12-19).

In this way, the Levites and priests were better provided for than anyone else. Keil and Delitzsch reckon that when Moses first established this law, the tribe of Levi contained 23,000 males, and therefore could hardly have included any more than 12,000 full grown men. Those 12,000 received the tithes of 600,000 Israelites; consequently, "one single Levite, without the slightest necessity for sowing, and without any of the expense of agriculture, reaped or received from the produce of the flocks and herds as much as five of the other Israelites." (J D Michaelis).

Keil and Delitzsch comment, however,

> "But this leaves out of sight the fact that tithes are never paid so exactly as this, and that no doubt there was as little conscientiousness in the matter then as there is at the present day, when those who are entitled to receive a tenth often receive less than a twentieth. Moreover, the revenue of the tribe, which the Lord had chosen as his own peculiar possession, was not intended to be a miserable and beggarly one; but it was hardly equal, at any time, to the revenues which the priestly castes of other nations derived from their endowments." [28]

On the payment of tithes to the Levites and the priests (and in circumstances that show this payment was often forgotten) see 2 Ch 31:5, 12, 19; Ne 12:44; etc.

Many passages in the church Fathers show that the early Christians accepted the O.T. law as a proper guide for Christian giving. Here are just two examples, from a 4th century document, *Apostolic Constitutions* -

> "For the Lord says to you in the Gospel: 'Unless your righteousness abound more than that of the scribes and Pharisees, ye shall by no means enter into the kingdom of heaven! Now herein will your righteousness exceed theirs, if you take greater care of the priests, the orphans, and the widows' ... So therefore

---

[28] *Commentary on the Old Testament*, <u>The Pentateuch</u>, Vol. III, pg 120; Eerdmans Publishing Co Grand Rapids, Michigan; 1976 reprint.

shalt thou do as the Lord has appointed, and shalt give to the priest what things are due to him." (Bk 2, ch 35.)

"All the first fruits of the winepress, the threshing floor, the oxen, and the sheep, shalt thou give to the priests, that thy storehouses and garners and the products of thy land may be blessed, and thou mayest be strengthened with corn and wine and oil, and the herds of thy cattle and flocks of thy sheep may be increased. Thou shalt give the tenth of thy increase to the orphan, and to the widow, and to the poor, and to the stranger. All the first fruits of thy hot bread, of thy barrels of wine, or oil, or honey, or nuts, or grapes, or the first fruits of other things, shalt thou give to the priests; but those of silver, and of garments, and of all sorts of possessions, to the orphan and to the widow." (Bk VII, ch 29.)

(ii) On the other hand, however, Deuteronomy 12 and 14 seem to indicate that tithes were to be used for ceremonial feasting. Three times each year, the Israelites were to gather *"before the Lord at the place that he would choose as a dwelling for his Name"* (De 16:6, 16).

On those occasions of celebration and rejoicing, they were to bring *"burnt offerings, sacrifices, tithes and special gifts"* (De 12:6) which the Hebrew men and their families were to eat before the Lord (12:7).

Some have seen these tithes as a "second" tithe, in addition to those given to the Levites. Evidence for this may be found in Josephus (Ant IV; 4:3), and also in the Apocrypha. Consider the following passage from Tobit (written c 450 BC):

"But I alone went often to Jerusalem for the feasts, as it is ordained for all Israel by an everlasting decree. Taking the first-fruits and the tithes of my produce and the first shearings, I would give these to the priests, the sons of Aaron, at the altar. Of all my produce I would give a tenth to the sons of Levi who ministered at Jerusalem; a second tenth I would sell, and I would go and spend the proceeds each year at Jerusalem; the third tenth I would give to those to whom it was my duty ..." (Tobit 1:6-8, RSV)

While the second and third tenths referred to here do not exactly meet the description of the tithes referred to in Deuteronomy 12, there are obvious similarities.

When we look closely at Deuteronomy 12 and 14, however, we find some difficulties with the idea of a "second" tithe, Deuteronomy 12:17 refers also to first-born animals - once these have been given, they can hardly be given again! Furthermore, 12:19 urges that the Levites be remembered - an unnecessary injunction, if they have already received tithes.

The answer seems to be that the people themselves could eat of the tithes when they brought them, but that the balance was to go to the Levites (see also De 14:22-27). This would then mean that the Levites and priests were not, in fact, as well off as suggested above.

Furthermore, Deuteronomy 14 talks of a special tithe every three years for the Levites, the aliens, the fatherless and the widows (14:28-29). Was this a "second" tithe, or even a "third" one? Probably not. It seems to mean simply that every third year, all the tithes would go to the people mentioned and that the givers would take nothing for themselves.

c. *The purpose of tithing*

To summarize, we can say that the purpose of tithing was threefold

- for religious worship and celebration

- for the support of the Levites

- for the care of the poor and needy.

The writers of the Proverbs have much to say about the need to be generous. He who keeps to himself will be the poorer, but he who shares will be richer (11:24-25). The person who gives to the poor is actually lending to God - who will repay him (19:17). It is God's blessing that brings wealth (10:22). A generous man will be blessed (22:9) and a hard worker will have abundant food (28:20). The ideal wife is one who "*opens her arms to the poor, and extends her hands to the needy*" (31:20).

Then, the prophet Malachi promises blessings on those who bring their tithes into God's storehouse (3:10 ff).

There are, in addition, scores of passages encouraging generosity, care for the needy, support of the Lord's house; etc. (Is 58:6 ff; Hg 1:1 ff; Am 5:11 ff; 5:25 ff; 6:1 ff; and many others).

1.3   NEW TESTAMENT GIVING

As in the Old Testament, the N.T. basis for giving is the fact that everything is God's anyway, and that when we give, we are simply returning to God what is already his (1 Co 3:21-23; 4:1-2; etc.).

a. *Tithing*

There are no N.T. injunctions that believers should tithe. Obviously, with the introduction of a New Covenant, the old system could not be retained as it was; however, there is much in the N.T. to encourage us to give generously.

b. *The nature of Christian giving* [29]

The most comprehensive N.T. passage on giving is found in 2 Corinthians, chapters eight and nine. There Paul shows that Christian giving is an expression of grace and love. So he points out that the Macedonian churches had already been given "grace," as a result of which they had been very generous (8:1-6). Hence he exhorts the Corinthians also to prove their grace (vs. 7) and love (vs. 8) in the same way. Jesus was the supreme example of this (vs. 9). Love always gives (remember Jn 3:16). Thus those who have much should share with those who have little (vs. 14-15), and so love is proven (vs. 24).

By contrast, there are at least five wrong attitudes in giving

- *the self righteous attitude*. These people are hoping to buy the favor of God by their gifts. Peter answered that idea bluntly enough -

"To hell with you and your money, because you thought you could buy the gift of God with money! You have no part or share in this ministry because your heart is not right before God!" (Ac 8:20-21).

Stern words! Yet quite literally, that is what the apostle said.

The Fathers had an equally dour view of the church receiving offerings from the unrighteous -

"The bishop ought to know whose oblations he ought to receive, and whose he ought not. For he is to avoid corrupt dealers, and not receive their gifts. 'For a corrupt dealer shall not be justified from sin' (Sir 26:19) ... He is also to avoid fornicators, for 'thou shalt not offer the hire of an harlot to the Lord' (De 23:18). He is also to avoid extortioners, and such as covet other men's goods, and adulterers: for the sacrifices of such as these are abominable with God. Also those that oppress

---

[29] The comments that follow under headings 1.2.b and c, were written by your editor, adding to and expanding material from the author's manuscript. Barry Chant resumes his full authorship in the next lesson.

the widow and overbear the orphan, and fill prisons with the innocent, and abuse their own servants wickedly, I mean with stripes, and hunger, and hard service, nay, destroy whole cities; do thou, O bishop, avoid such as these, and their odious oblations. Thou shalt also refuse rogues, and such pleaders that plead on the side of injustice, and idol-makers, and thieves, and unjust publicans, and those that deceive by false balances and deceitful measures, and a soldier who is a false accuser and not content with his wages, but does violence to the needy, or murderer, a cut-throat, and an unjust judge, a subverter of causes, him that lies in wait for men, a worker of abominable wickedness, a drunkard, a blasphemer, a sodomite, an usurer, and every one that is wicked and opposes the will of God. For the scripture says that all such as these are abominable with God ... Avoid therefore such ministrations, as you would the price of a dog and the hire of an harlot; for both of them are forbidden by the laws ... (If) the prophets of God did not admit of presents from the impious, it is reasonable, O bishops, that neither should you." [30]

- *the idolatrous attitude*. These people reckon that money is the chief goal of life, the source of all happiness. They keep as much as they can. They give as little as they can. They cannot conceive that happiness is possible without an abundance of material possessions.

- *the carnal attitude*. For these people, money is the source of their security. They would like to give generously to the church and to the poor; but they are afraid to give, for they fear being left destitute. They have no confidence that God is able to keep his promise (Ps 37:25; Mt 6:28-33).

- *the dutiful attitude*. These people give well to the work of God, and regularly, but mainly out of habit. Their giving has become a ritual, it lacks any true spiritual dynamic, or any input of faith. Such mechanistic giving cannot attract a divine response.

- *the punitive attitude*. These people find prosperity an embarrassment; they feel they do not deserve any good thing in life, but rather they deserve to suffer. So they give to make amends for sin, to punish themselves. They give more than they should in order to keep

---

[30] *Apostolic Constitutions*, Bk IV, Ch 6 & 7. From *The Ante-Nicene Fathers*, Vol. VII; Eerdmans Publishing Co, Grand Rapids, Michigan; 1979 reprint.

themselves at the level of poverty they believe is their proper condition. Their giving has an appearance of piety, but it is really far removed from the grace of God.

c. *Two basic principles*

(i) Giving must be obedient

(a) You should ask God what he wants you to give. Many people are reluctant to do this, because they are sure God will ask them to give more than they are willing to surrender. But note:

1. It is foolish to give less than God demands, because he will in any case eventually get what he wants, plus a "late" penalty (cp. Le 27:14-30, and other similar references, where the law of God insisted that the promised sum must be paid, plus an increment of 20 per cent, which was imposed as compensation for withholding the original oblation).

2. It is unnecessary to give more than God wants. You cannot increase the blessing of God in your life merely by giving more money, any more than a farmer can increase his harvest merely by jamming more seed into the same piece of earth (in fact, too much seed may jeopardize his entire crop). God says, "*I prefer obedience to sacrifice*" (1 Sa 15:22).

You should realize that God is really not interested in your money (Ps 50:9-15); but he is deeply interested in *you*. He wants you to give, not for his sake, not because he needs your money, but for *your* sake, because you *need* to give in order to perfect your own character. Giving is a tool that the Lord uses to bring you to maturity, to work righteousness in you, to develop tougher faith.

That is why it is important to develop a sensitive obedience to the Holy Spirit in your giving. You will simply frustrate the deeper purpose of God if you give too much or too little. That is also why you cannot use your neighbor as a guide in your giving. The purpose of God differs in both of you. That purpose may require your neighbor to give much and you little, or the reverse.

(b) However, as a general guide, you may suppose that the Lord will always direct you at least to give:

1. to the church

Most believers today feel that tithing is still a good practice. As shown above, it antedates Moses and seems to find its origin in love rather than law. Paul expresses this principle of love very clearly -

> *"Each person should give what he has decided in his heart to give, not reluctantly, nor under compulsion, for God lives a cheerful giver"* (2 Co 9:7; and cp. Ac 11:29).

And what we give should be done voluntarily - indeed, cheerfully (Greek: *hilaros*) - that is, given freely, with no sense of compulsion.

Love, then, has replaced law as the prime motivation for giving. And most would feel that the level of giving ruled by love could hardly be less than the level ruled by law. Nonetheless, in the church no-one should be *"hard-pressed"* through giving (2 Co 8:13). Even in the case of Ananias and Sapphira, the problem was not that they did not give all, for they had a right to give whatever they liked, but that they were dishonest about it (Ac 5:4).

It would seem wise, however, to establish a regular pattern of giving (cp. 1 Co 16:1-4), and to make this a basis on which to build. Special appeals may still be made from time to time (cp. 2 Co 8 & 9). But in general you should respond only to appeals that come from approved sources. Not all appeals are genuine. Notice how careful Paul was to ensure that approved representatives of the churches handled his appeal for help for the Jerusalem saints (1 Co 16:3,4; 2 Co 8:16 ff; cp. Ac 11:19-30).

---

* **Think Spot**: *Many believers work on the basis of giving their regular "tithe" exclusively to their local church, but giving additional "offerings" to missionaries, evangelists, par.-church bodies, etc. What do you think of that?*

The basic reason that requires Christians to give regularly to the church is the support of the ministry. A clear principle is laid down in the N.T. that *"the workman deserves his wages."* So Jesus told the seventy that they should not be reluctant to accept hospitality from their hearers (Lu 10:7).

Paul establishes the same principle in 1 Ti 5:17-18 and 1 Co 9:7 ff. He declares that those who preach and teach the gospel have the right to live from it as well (see 1 Co 9:14). He puts it simply to the Galatians when he says that those who receive spiritual benefit from their teachers should return material benefit to them (Ga 6:6). While Paul himself at times refused to claim that right, he did not deny that it existed (see 1 Co 9:12-23).

> *   **Think Spot**: *What order of precedence do you think Paul would have given to the following appeals - pastor's stipend, building fund, TV programs, publishing, missions, a resident or itinerant teacher, prophet, evangelist?*

2. to missions

The missionary mandate is the primary task given by Christ to his church (Mt 28:18-20; Mk 16:15-20; Ac 1:8; etc.). It cannot be imagined, then, that Christian giving can ignore missions, both home and foreign. The obedient Christian will surely devote a regular and significant part of his giving to the task of spreading the gospel around the world, and to supporting ministry outside of his local church.

3. to the poor

See Ps 41:1-3; Pr 19:17; etc. As in O.T. days, so in the N.T., giving to the poor is seen as being in a sense giving to God. So Jesus taught that what we do to the least of his brothers we are in effect doing to him (Mt 25:31-46).

The major thrust of 2 Co 8 & 9 is the need for the Greek and Macedonian churches to help the saints in Jerusalem who were in great need (1 Co 16:1-4; 2 Co 8:1- 4). Other passages indicate a similar concern - Ga 2:10; 1 Ti 5:16; He 13:16; Ja 2:14-16; 1 Jn 3:16-18.

> *   **Think Spot**: *Do you, does your church, accept the responsibility for the poor that scripture enjoins upon all Christians? Does this responsibility include all the poor, or only those who are in the church?*

(c) As I have already indicated, you may also suppose that all Christian giving should be characterized by a spirit of warm and cheerful generosity. The Spirit of God is not likely to bid you to give parsimoniously, nor coldly and indifferently. Yet do not allow your giving to be controlled by sentiment, nor by a merely emotional response to some appeal, nor even by the fear of being accused of giving too little. Rather, let it be a planned, disciplined, and obedient response to what you perceive to be the will of God for you.

(ii) Giving must be an act of faith

If there should be a greatness about your *giving to* God, there should also be a greatness about your *getting from* God. When people say that they want to give to God, but don't want anything in return, they reveal, not piety, but pride. It is true that we should expect nothing back from other people whom we are helping; but we should certainly expect a return from God (see Lu 6:35).

So you should give with positive anticipation of a divine response to your giving. The promise of God will not work just of its own accord. It must be made by faith to work. Two spiritual laws come into effect here:

(a) *The law of proportionate return* (Lu 6:38)

Twice Christ says in effect, "*Give and you will get!*" He implies that the measure of your getting will be determined by the measure of your *giving*. Notice -

1. Christ endorses the value of money. He is not embarrassed by it. He knows that you need it. He knows that the church needs it. It is not a dirty word. He understands, as you should, that your money, and the way you handle it, is a vital part of your spiritual life and of your relationship with God. In fact, if you fail here, you can hardly succeed in any other part of your walk with God (Lu 16:10-11).

2. Christ leaves no room for fear. He commands, "*Give,*" and his promise, "*You will receive,*" remains unchanged whether the times are good or bad. So refuse to allow your faith to be dominated by the state of the national economy, or by your personal need. Locate your supply in God, not in your employer, nor in your banker, nor in any human source (cp. Ps 37:25; 34:10-11).

Too often when the headlines are gloomy, people become anxious and tighten their purse strings. Just when they most need to be released in their spirit, to be bold in faith in the matter of giving, they become fearful and parsimonious!

But did God give his promise only so it could sit uselessly in scripture during good times? Or does the promise belong especially to the hour of financial crisis? Surely the promises of God relating to giving and receiving are more necessary to you in bad times than they are in good times! If money is short, perhaps you should increase, not lessen, your giving? Perhaps the best thing a man could do who had only one dollar left would be to turn it into ten cent pieces, and start giving them away in the name of the Lord, to the church, to missions, to the poor! Poverty, after all, is a state of mind more than it is a fiscal state. It is not more money you need, but more faith.

3. Christ leaves you no room just to amass treasure for yourself. The word "give" is imperative. Remember that God hates hoarders (Mt 6:19-21).

4. Christ promises more than a merely equal return. He actually promises *"good measure, pressed down, shaken together, running over."* That is what you should expect from him.

*   Think Spot: This law of proportionate return is sometimes expressed, not as "give and you will receive," but "give so that you will receive." What is the difference?

(b) The law of sowing and reaping (2 Co 9:6-10)

Notice:

- God wants you to have a surplus; he is able to provide for you abundantly (vs. 8-9); he recognizes that you cannot be obedient to the command to give unless you have money available to give.

- God provides this need through the law of sowing and reaping (vs. 6, 10).

- you must *"make up your mind"* (vs. 7) what you intend to do in response to this law -

1. What is in your mind as you give your offering to the church week by week? If you give perfunctorily, without concern, with your mind on other matters, then perhaps you are not giving enough. You should at least give enough, so that it hurts enough, so that you care enough about your gift to want to pray that God will use it to

enhance your prosperity and the prosperity of the church. In any case, your mind should be fixed upon the act of giving, and you should always surround the oblation with believing prayer. It should be a conscious act of worship, not an indifferent religious duty.

2. You should view your gift as seed planted for a harvest. This removes any suspicion of greed or selfishness. You become like a farmer who, by merely putting seed into the ground, cannot compel the earth to yield its harvest; but he can co-operate with the earth, conform to the laws of harvest, and so expect a rich return. Just so, you cannot demand nor buy the blessing of God, merely because you have given money; but you can sow seed for a harvest, with obedience and faith.

3. This harvest principle is declared in many places - Pr 3:9-10; 11:24-25; etc. The successful outworking of this principle brings glory to God (2 Co 9:12-15).

1.4 CONCLUSION

Generous giving and generous getting belong together in the church; the one cannot exist without the other. A giving and no getting = poverty. All getting and no giving = greed. You should expect to give more to God, and then to get more, so that you can give more, and get more, to give more ... Notice though that the process begins and ends with giving. You give so that, by receiving more, you can enlarge your giving, over and over again. Getting is not the goal, but giving.

2. THE SACRAMENTS [31]

Roman Catholics reckon that there are seven sacraments: *baptism, confirmation, the Eucharist, penance, extreme unction, holy orders, and matrimony.* Protestants reckon there are but two sacraments: *baptism and holy communion.*

Who is right?

It would take a braver man than I to give a firm answer to that question! But I will venture a few opinions, hoping they will not be too far from either scripture or truth.

---

[31] Your editor is the sole author of section 6, "The Sacraments" (Barry Chant's authorship is resumed in the next lesson.)

The word "sacrament" does not occur in scripture. However, it is linked with the N.T. through the Latin word *sacramentum* which was used to translate the Greek word *musterion* (Mt 13:11; Ro 11:25; 1 Co 2:7; Ep 1:9; 3:3-4; Cl 1:26-27; etc.). Unfortunately, *sacramentum* was not a good translation of *musterion*, and it introduced into the church ideas that go beyond the meaning of the Greek word. I want to trace this development.

Musterion is used in the N.T. to describe God's great plan of salvation, which for many centuries was hidden, but is now made known to the church through the preaching of the Word. This plan is called a "mystery" both because it was hidden for so long, and because even now it can be discovered only by those to whom the Holy Spirit gives understanding.

However, during its journey from *musterion* to *sacramentum*, the idea of "mystery" became attached not just to the gospel, but even more to the means by which the gospel was proclaimed in the church. The first of those means was, of course, the Word, and the beginnings of the process that attached the idea of "mystery" to the Word can already be seen in Ep 3:3-6 and Cl 1:25-28. But it was not long before the same idea began to be attached to any observance that revealed some aspect of salvation, or that created some kind of encounter with the risen Christ. The two most notable examples were naturally baptism and the Eucharist, but other things were easily included, such as the laying on of hands (He 6:1-2), anointing with oil (Ja 5:14-15), even Christian matrimony (Ep 5:31-32, notice Paul's use of *musterion*).

Nonetheless *musterion* was not fully taken over by "sacramentum," nor did it receive the kind of definitive or technical sense that it now has, until almost the fourth century. In other words, for at least two hundred years the church did not sense any need to adopt a collective term to describe a particular group of its ordinances. If you had asked those early Christians whether there were two "sacraments," or seven, they would not have known what you were talking about. This indicates that the term "sacrament," as we use it, is rather artificial, and the quarrel about how many "sacraments" there are seems to be needless.

So against the Protestant contention that there are only two sacraments, the objection may be raised that the N.T. itself describes more than two agents through which the Holy Spirit reveals the mystery of Christ to the church. But then the Catholic list of seven sacraments seems to be just as arbitrary (unless of course it is allowed that the church does have authority to make such lists and to impose them upon all of its members).

Why specify either two sacraments, or seven, when neither scripture nor the early church found it necessary to be so definite on the subject? It is difficult to escape the feeling that the whole quarrel would vanish if the various antagonists would simply drop the word "sacrament" (with its hoary and largely unbiblical accretions) and return to the more open statements of scripture.

That seems an unlikely prospect. So we shall have to continue using the word. But first, we must decide what it means, and what things it belongs to.

2.1 THE MEANING OF "SACRAMENT"

There are two main ideas about the meaning of "sacrament:" that it describes a *channel* of grace; or, that it describes a *sign* of grace.

In the first view, the worshiper actually encounters Christ in the sacrament, and receives an infusion of the life of Christ - that is, the grace of God is conveyed to the worshiper through the sacrament.

In the second view, the sacrament has an exclusively symbolic or memorial purpose - that is, there is no conveyance of grace.

The peril inherent in the first view is that the sacrament may become an end in itself, that the attention of the worshiper will be wholly focused on the sacrament, rather than on Christ, without whom the sacrament is void. The peril inherent in the second view is to reduce the sacrament to a perfunctory observance, stripping it of any really useful or gracious function in the church, and making it redundant to a full Christian life. Both perils have been too often realized.

a. Sacraments do not lie at the heart of the church. That place belongs to the Word - see 1 Co 1:17-18, 21; Ep 5:26; Cl 1:5-6; Ro 10:17; He 6:5; 1 Pe 1:23-25; Re 19:13; etc.

It is clear that the Word can and does exist without the sacraments; but sacraments have no meaning apart from the Word. The sacraments exist only because the Word commands them and gives them life. Again, the Word is essential for salvation, so that since Adam not one soul has been saved apart from the Word; but the sacraments are not so, and many people have entered the kingdom of God without them. Not that the Word itself saves. Christ is the Savior. But Christ is made known through the Word; hence the apostle did not hesitate to associate the Word with the *musterion* of the gospel (cp. Ep 3:3-6; Cl 1:25-28).

b. Sacraments are most likely to become objects of magical superstition when the Word is denied its preeminent place. So long as the church maintains the centrality of the Word, no sacrament can be given an undue prominence, and the faith of the people will retain its proper focus - that is, it will remain fixed on Christ, who is revealed in the Word.

Foremost in the church stands Christ (He 2:12; Re 1:12-13); proximate to Christ is the Word, revealed by the Holy Spirit, and proclaimed by the messengers of God (Ro 10:8, 14-17; 1 Co 2:9-11); then, only then, come all other ordinances in the church. (The psalmist expressed the supremacy of the Word in his striking exclamation: *"You have exalted your Word even above your Name!"* - Ps 138:2.)

c. In order to establish the primacy of the Word, it has been God's common practice throughout history to add certain attesting "signs" to his Word. Those signs have been of two sorts: ceremonial and charismatic. The signs are given for a double purpose: to confirm the Word supernaturally, and to convey it visibly to the people.

Confirming the Word is primarily the task of the charismatic signs (cp. Mk 16:20 ; He 2:3-4; etc.).

Conveying the Word is primarily the task of the ceremonial signs (cp. 1 Co 11:26; He 9:8; etc.).

I use the description "primarily," because the functions of the two groups of signs do overlap to some extent. In other words, the charismatic signs may provide a visible demonstration of the Word in action, and a revelation of Christ, as well as fulfilling their ordinary task of supernaturally confirming the truth of the Word. That is, they may preach as well as perform.

Likewise, the ceremonial signs may be a means by which the power of Christ is supernaturally brought to the church, in addition to fulfilling their ordinary task of providing a visual picture of the message the Word contains. That is, they may perform as well as preach.

The idea of "mystery" is associated with both sets of signs: the charismatic (cp. 1 Co 14:2); and the ceremonial (cp. Mt 26:29 with 13:11). Hence the description "sacrament" may be applied to both sets, for they were both intended by God to be a means by which the church could (1) enhance its fellowship with him; (2) sharpen its vision of Christ; (3) experience his life and power; and (4) share in the drama of Christ's death and resurrection.

Thus far we have traced the following development: the idea of "mystery" (or of sacrament) began with the divine plan of salvation; then it passed on to the Word that revealed the plan; and then, because they are a means of proclaiming that Word, and/or of conveying its power to the church, the charismatic and ceremonial signs also became identified with the "mystery."

d. But then something went wrong. The charismata began to vanish from the church, leaving a vacuum in witness and experience that had to be occupied. That vacuum was filled by the ceremonies (notably baptism and the Eucharist), which became for many people the only possible source of the kind of supernatural experiences that had formerly been brought to them by the charismata. The ceremonies were thus required to support a burden much heavier than the one given them in the simple words of scripture.

e. Because the ceremonies had now become the prime means of realizing the Word within the church, they were said to encompass the "mystery" of the gospel in a special way. That is, they took on a special character of "sacredness." They were thought of as belonging peculiarly to God. Thus the early Latin-speaking church changed *musterion to sacramentum.*

There is a subtle and emotive difference in the meaning of those two words. *Musterion* (as mentioned above) was originally used in secular Greek to describe the various "mystery" cults, along with their secret religious and political teachings. In the N.T. it means simply "the secret thoughts, plans, and dispensations of God, which are hidden from human reason ... and hence must be revealed to those for whom they are intended" (Arndt and Gingrich). In that sense, the word occurs more than 20 times in the N.T., and it is applied to many different things.

Sacramentum, however, originally meant "a deposit placed before the gods" - hence it was used to describe an object that was reckoned to be specially sacred, being owned, as it were, by the gods, and therefore jealously guarded by them. A *sacramentum* possessed a uniquely divine quality. The word conveyed a more strongly sacrosanct feeling than did *musterion.* It induced a deeper sense of awe and reverence. That which formerly was valued because it contained the "mystery" of the gospel, was now revered as an object "sacred" in itself.

f. From the belief that certain ceremonies (or "sacraments") were highly sacred, and that they had a peculiar capacity to reveal Christ, it was a short step to the idea that these sacred ceremonies were actually replete with grace. Even more, not only was grace deposited in the sacraments, but those sacraments could in fact cause grace to appear in the worshiper, without reference to that person's life. In other words, unless the worshiper deliberately erected a mental or spiritual barrier against the sacraments, it was believed they would automatically convey the grace of God to him.

g. Thus the sacraments became sources of divine grace, independently of the Word, and indeed soon surpassed the Word in importance. They even began to usurp the place of Christ. The vision of a risen and glorified Christ became lost in a concept of a fleshly Christ, who was more or less imprisoned within the sacraments, and who was accessible to Christians only through those sacraments.

That sorry development was most observable in the celebration of the Eucharist during the Middle Ages. The priests, in the minds of a superstitious populace, [32] became like magicians who possessed an awesome ability to change bread and wine into flesh and blood. The priests were even thought to have the power to control the unseen world, both supernal and infernal, to be able to command both heaven and hell.

Against such medieval superstitions the Reformers vigorously protested. They rightly insisted that the Holy Spirit cannot be controlled by any man, and neither can the grace of God be commanded. They restored the biblical emphasis: sacraments are given to serve the Word of God; sacraments have no validity apart from the Word of God; sacraments are effective only when the participant is striving to obey God and believes the promise of God; sacraments belong to those, and only to those, who have entered into a personal relationship with Christ.

Such an insistence on true worship and faith is the one thing that can separate a genuine sacramental observance from one that is merely magical. The sacraments do not get their virtue from the various elements of water, wine, bread, oil, and the like, nor from priestly craft, nor from ritual actions.

---

[32] But not necessarily in the minds of the better leaders and more noble spirits in the church, many of whom held firmly to more scriptural views.

Their virtue comes solely from the gracious activity of the Holy Spirit, who fulfills the promise of God and himself conveys grace to every person who participates in them with repentance, faith, true love, and sincere worship (Ro 5:5; 14:17; 15:13, 16; 1 Th 1:5; Tit 3:5; He 6:4-6; Ep 4:30; etc.).

h. However, even if we grant that the Word and the Spirit are the true source of divine grace, the question still remains: in what way, if any, do the sacraments provide a channel of that grace to the worshiper? And another question: which observances in the church should we call "sacraments?" In other words, how many sacraments are there, and in what way do they benefit the church?

2.2   How Many Sacraments?

My answer to this question has already been partly given. It seems inescapable, from the broad way *musterion* is used in the N.T., that there are a number of observances and/or practices, found both in public worship and in private devotion, that possess a sacramental quality (that is, they are somehow identified with the "mystery" of the gospel).

It also seem inescapable that the argument about the number of sacraments is not affected by the issue of whether or not they are channels of grace. In other words, if it is believed that grace is channeled through one scripturally commanded observance, then it is not difficult to believe that grace can be channeled through all such observances - whether baptism, the Eucharist, laying on of hands, anointing with oil, singing "psalms, hymns, and spiritual songs," and so on. Likewise, any argument that can be used to deny a conveyance of grace by one observance (say, the Eucharist), is equally effective against all of the others.

So, leaving aside for the moment the grace issue, and sticking to the N.T. use of *musterion*, it seems valid to say two things -

a. There are several observances that may be called sacraments, but the number is probably indeterminate. Thus Latourette, describing the church in the 15th century writes:

> "Much of the religious life of the laity centered in the sacraments . . . It was not until 1439 that their number was finally officially fixed. Some authors revered by the Church had spoken of only two, baptism and the Eucharist. Peter Damien (11th century) had enumerated twelve, and Hugo of St. Victor (12th

century) thirty. Peter Lombard (12th century seems to have been the first to limit them to seven and to give the list which the Roman Catholic church eventually made final." [33]

The same author writes elsewhere -

"Before the year 500 the exact nature of the sacraments had not been given clear authoritative interpretation, nor had the number been fixed. What there was in the Middle Ages which led to more precise official definition is not certain. Perhaps it was the prominence given the miraculous. After a discussion which lasted for several centuries, the number was officially decreed to be seven - by the Council of Florence in 1439." [34]

If the number of sacraments has to be set, after centuries of debate, by a decree of the church, it is clear that there is insufficient evidence to resolve the matter from scripture alone. Which means, if one is unwilling to accept that 15th century decree, the matter should be left unresolved.

b. However, among those several observances there are two that are given special prominence: baptism and the Eucharist.

Those two stand apart from the others because they are uniquely associated with Calvary. In a manner that none of the other observances can imitate, baptism and the Eucharist present the passion of Christ. Other observances undoubtedly gain their value from the cross, but unlike baptism and the Eucharist they do not specifically portray Christ's death and resurrection.

Christ himself suggested this special link between his passion and those two sacraments, by his enigmatic question to the sons of Zebedee -

"Are ye able to drink of the cup that I shall drink of, and to be baptized with the baptism that I am baptized with?" (Mt 20:22, KJV; see also Ro 6:3-4; 1 Co 11:23-26).

The primary reason among Protestants for recognizing only two sacraments, baptism and the Eucharist, is because those two have no meaning or use outside of their association with Calvary and their portrayal of the passion of Christ. By contrast, other possible sacraments do not have that special identification with the cross. They may depend upon the

---

[33] K. S. Latourette, *A History of Christianity*; Harper & Row, New York, 1975; pg. 528.
[34] *A History of the Expansion of Christianity*, Vol. 2, "The Thousand Years of Uncertainty;" Zondervan Publishing House, Grand Rapids, Michigan, 1970; pg. 423.

cross for their validity, but they are not figures of it. So, without denying the possibility that other ordinances or practices may rightly be called sacraments, it does seem fair to place baptism and the Eucharist in a special category, and to recognize that they are sacraments in a preeminent sense.

2.3 WHAT BENEFITS DO THEY BRING?

If churchly dogmatics and decrees are ignored, it seems unnecessary to believe either that the sacraments are symbols only, with no power to convey the grace of God to a worshiper, or that they are supernaturally full of the grace of God, which is automatically conveyed to anyone who receives them.

It is evident from scripture that the power of God, both to heal and to destroy, is associated with the sacraments (1 Co 11:27-32; 10:14-22; Ac 22:16; 1 Co 6:11; He 10:22; etc.).

It is equally evident (as I have shown above), that the sacraments do not have power merely because they are observed.

Whatever capacity they have to convey grace to the recipient arises from two sources:

a. the preaching of the Word, which brings Christ to the people;

b. a believing and worshipful response to the Word by those who receive the sacraments.

Without the Word and personal faith, the sacraments are either rendered futile or become a channel, not of grace, but of divine judgment (1 Co 11:27, 30).

Those, then, who are baptized in trustful obedience to the command of Christ should expect to encounter the resurrection life of Christ as they emerge from the water, and their baptism should bring them into a new and higher dimension of Christian life (Ro 6:5-11; Cl 2:12).

Likewise, those who celebrate the Eucharist should do so with repentance and faith, knowing there is a real presence of Christ at the table (in the bread and in the cup), and that worthy eating and drinking will convey to them the healing grace of Christ (1 Co 10:16). [35]

---

[35] Since scripture makes no attempt to explain in what way Christ is present in the Eucharist, or in any other sacrament, neither will I.

But let no one imagine that he or she can observe any sacrament carelessly, without repentance, or in unbelief, and expect to receive anything from God except wrath (cp. Jude vs. 11-13). No sacrament has power in itself to save anybody. Salvation comes from Christ and is given to those who receive and believe his Word (1 Jn 5:6-12). Sacraments have power only when the Holy Spirit acts in and through them to convey divine grace to those who through the sacraments show their confidence in the Word and their love for Christ. [36]

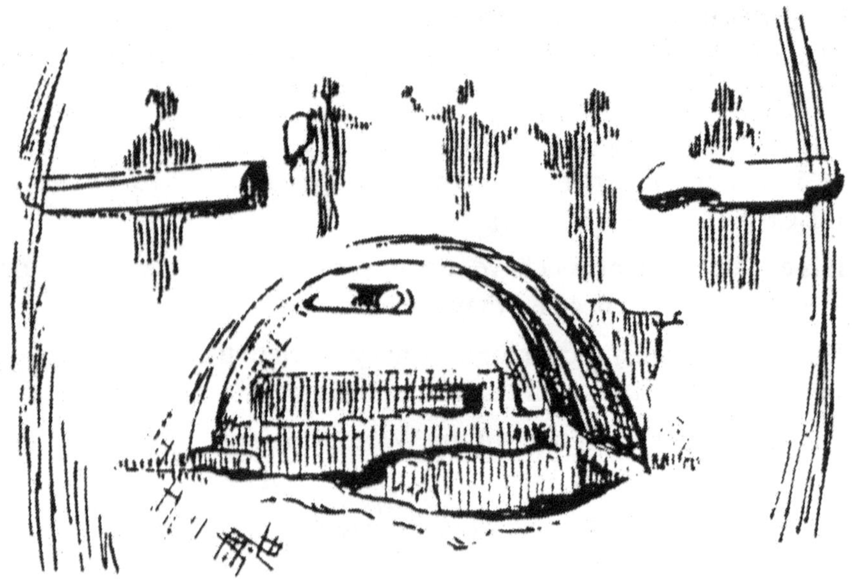

The Crypt of the Five Virgins in the Roman Catacombs.

---

[36] You should note that the grace channeled through the sacraments is not some special sacramental grace, different from any other. It is the regular grace of God that springs out of Calvary. The sacraments are simply special channels of that grace, a special means by which that grace can be conveyed to the worshiper. It is, however, possible that they do add to that grace a dimension which may not be so readily available from some other source.

LESSON TEN

THE CHURCH AND THE KINGDOM

INTRODUCTION

Many books on church growth have been published in recent years, most of which contain excellent material. As we have seen in an earlier lesson, such books need to consider the subject historically, culturally and scripturally. Such a treatment is beyond the scope of this study. All we can do here is briefly examine how churches were planted in the first century. The application of this to the twentieth and twenty-first centuries will be largely up to you.

It could be said that some of the major ingredients in successful church management are -

> Message
>
> Men (i.e. leadership)
>
> Members
>
> Machinery (i.e. equipment etc.)
>
> Money
>
> Methods
>
> Marketing (i.e. promotion and evangelism)

We have already studied some of these (Men, Members, Money). In this section we shall look at three others - Message, Methods, Marketing. [37]

(I) PLANTING NEW CHURCHES

1.   THE MESSAGE

A study of the preaching of the early church shows a remarkable uniformity of message: it was Christ crucified and raised from the dead.

---

[37] Barry Chant resumes full authorship with this lesson.

An examination of the preaching of Peter, John, Stephen, Philip, Paul and others shows the following frequently mentioned elements:

- Jesus as the Messiah of prophecy.

- Jesus' signs and wonders.

- Jesus' crucifixion.

- Jesus' resurrection.

- Jesus' second coming.

- the need to repent, believe and be baptized.

- the promise of the Holy Spirit.

(See Ac 2:14 ff; 3:11 ff; 5:29 ff; 7:1 ff; 8:5; 8:30 ff; 10:34 ff; 13:16 ff; 17:22 ff; 26:1 ff; 1 Co 15:3-8).

On two occasions, Paul talks mainly about God being the Creator of the world and all that is in it. The first was at Lystra, where there was a special problem (Ac 14:14 ff). The second was at Athens, where he was debating with philosophers; but even here, his primary focus was on the resurrection (Ac 17:16 ff; notice especially vs. 18, 31).

Overall, the preaching of the work of Christ in redemption was clearly central to all apostolic preaching. Indeed, it is interesting that the early preachers seemed to say little about the teaching of Jesus when they preached the gospel. This seems to have been kept more for the believers. Note 1 Co 2:1-3 and 15:3-8, which seem to give regular patterns of preaching.

---

* **Think Spot**: *What are the implications of the above for twentieth century evangelism? (Consider the facts that we live in a different culture and in a community that already pays lip service to Jesus' redemptive work - does this make any difference?)*

Finally, it is interesting to note that from the days of John the Baptist, the key message was the proclamation of the Kingdom of God. John the Baptist (Mt 3:1-2); Jesus (Mk 1:15); the disciples (Lu 10:11); Peter (Ac 2:30 ff); Philip (8:12); Paul (14:22; 19:8; 20:25; 28:31) all proclaimed the coming of the Kingdom.

2.   THE METHODS

An examination of apostolic methods of evangelism is revealing. Consider the following:

2.1   THE EVANGELISTS

There are a few references to "every-believer evangelism." Thus, when the Jerusalem Church was persecuted, it was *"the believers"* who went everywhere preaching, while the apostles remained in the city (Ac 8:1-4). Hence, Philip evangelized Samaria (8:5 ff) and some others (who are unnamed) took the message to Antioch (11:19) - a move that was to have long range effects.

However, the overwhelming impression one gains from the N.T. is that evangelism was not done by the rank and file but by the apostles and evangelists. Apart from the two places mentioned, all the other churches seem to have been founded as the result of missionary work by Peter (e.g. Caesarea - Ac 10:1ff) or Paul (e.g. Pisidian, Antioch, Iconium, Lystra, Derbe, Philippi; etc. - 13:1 ff) or Barnabas (15:39); etc. So Philip also was later recognized as an evangelist (21:8), not just as a "believer."

Furthermore, there is a remarkable absence of emphasis on personal evangelism in the N.T. epistles. The major thrust there is on living - living an upright life and so bearing witness to Christ (e.g. Ph 2:14 ff). Even a cursory glance at the N.T. shows that the strong emphasis is on relationships, uprightness, perseverance, faithfulness, and the like. Consider the repetition in Titus, for instance, of phrases like *"doing what is good"* (2:7; 2:14; 3:8; 3:14); in Ephesians, on Christ-like character (4:20-32; 5:1 ff; 6:1 ff); in Peter, on humility and love (1 Pe 2:21 ff; 3:8 ff; 4:1 ff); and in James, on practical Christian living (especially chapter 2).

It is hard to escape the conclusion that it was essentially by their *lives* that N.T. Christians witnessed to their faith. The actual preaching seems to have been done mainly by those with ministry gifts.

---

*   **Think Spot**: *Could it be that N.T. Christians were all so good at witnessing that there was no need for the writers to exhort them to do it? Someone recently claimed that only 10% of any local church are likely to be evangelists - do you agree?*

2.2   THE LOCATION

Where did N.T. evangelism take place? The answer is simple - anywhere at all! Hence, the following are some of the places used:

> The Temple courts (Ac 2:46; 3:1 ff; 5:12)
>
> Homes (2:46; 20:20)
>
> The Sanhedrin (6:15-7:56; 23:1 ff)
>
> Public places (8:4 ff)
>
> A desert (8:26 ff)
>
> A large house (10:24, 27; 11:11)
>
> The Synagogues (13:5; 13:14; 13:44; 14:1)
>
> A market place (or some similar public place - 14:8 ff)
>
> A public place of prayer (16:13 ff)
>
> A prison (16:16 ff)
>
> A market place (17:17)
>
> The Areopagus (a law court named after a hill, 17:22)
>
> A lecture hall (19:9)
>
> An upstairs room (20:8)
>
> The steps of a Roman barracks (21:30 ff)
>
> One's own home (28:30-31)

It can readily be seen that the apostles simply used any convenient or suitable location for presenting the gospel.

It should be noted, however, that their major aim was to be where the people were - and also, to have a point of identification with them. Hence, Paul's use of the synagogues, homes, and lecture halls - familiar meeting places where religion was already a point of interest (cp. 1 Co. 9:19 ff. See also Ac 16:1-3).

---

*   **Think Spot**: *Where are the best places for evangelism in the land today? Would Paul have had a TV program or magazine?*

2.3   THE APPROACH

As we have seen, the message was Christ crucified and risen.

With the Jews, the approach was clearly to go to the synagogues and to attempt to prove from the Scriptures that Jesus was the Christ (e.g. Ac 17:2 ff; 17:10 ff).

With the Gentiles, the starting point was a general belief in God, leading to a presentation of Christ as God's Son and Savior (e.g. Ac 10:34 ff; 14:14 ff; 17:22 ff. Note also how Paul approached the first believers in Ephesus, using John's ministry as a point of contact - 19:1 ff).

So again we see an attempt to start on common ground wherever possible.

Furthermore, we can see that the apostles were just as much at home with the individual (Ac 8:26 ff) or a small group (16:32 ff) as with a large crowd (2:40-41; 6:7; 8:5 ff; 14:11 ff). Indeed, large crowds do not seem to have been the regular pattern. It is clear that in many cases only a few turned to the Lord, and the

2.4   THE ABILITY

No method has value unless it works! When you are dealing with a divine message, you need divine power to confirm its truth. The effectiveness of the preaching of the early church was due to its supernatural attestation (Mk 16:20; Ac 5:12; Ro 15:18-19; He 2:3-4).

a. *The name of Jesus*

All preaching, teaching, healing, deliverance, etc. was carried out *"in Jesus' name."* That does not necessarily mean those actual words were used (a popular misconception), but that the early disciples saw their authority and right to minister as stemming from Jesus' name. So only through his name can one be saved (Ac 2:21; 4:12) and healing is in his name (3:16; 4:7, 10). Baptism (2:38; 19:5), preaching (5:28, 40), deliverance (Mk 16:17; Ac 16:18), suffering (9:16; 15:26; 21:13), etc. are all in the name of Jesus.

b. *The Holy Spirit*

There are literally dozens of references to the power of the Spirit in Acts. An exhaustive analysis would be a study in its own right. The following points can be made here -

From the very beginning of Acts we see how Jesus gave instructions *"through the Holy Spirit to the apostles"* (1:2); how he promised they would be baptized in the Spirit (1:5); and how that by the Spirit, they would be his witnesses to the ends of the earth (1:8). Then, the story of the church is really launched with the outpouring of the Spirit at Pentecost (2:1ff). The power of the Spirit is clearly the major factor in the early church's witness, evangelism, and growth.

So the first 3,000 converts are won at Pentecost (Ac 2:41). Then, filled with the Spirit, the apostles bear witness (4:8; 4:31; 5:32; 6:3, 5, 10; 7:55; 9:17, 31; 13:52 etc.). So it is the Spirit who guides (8:26, 39; 11:12; 16:6 ff), who empowers (1:8; 6:8; 13:9), who gives wisdom to the church (15:28), who appoints leaders (20:28), who inspires prophets (21:10-11), and so on. It has been suggested, in fact, that the book might better be called *"Acts of the Holy Spirit"* (although this would not be truly correct, either, since the Spirit only acts through people who willingly co-operate with him).

A study of the epistles would yield a similar wealth of references to the work of the Spirit in the continuing life of the churches.

c. *Faith*

Only by faith can anything lasting be achieved for God. Hence, those who first planted churches were also men and women of faith. It was faith, along with the power of the Spirit and the authority of the name of Jesus, that brought healing to the lame man at the temple (Ac 3:16). Stephen was full of faith and the Spirit (6:5), as also was Barnabas (11:24).

Jesus taught that signs and wonders would result from faith (Mk 16:17-18). The early Christians were taught that only by faith was it possible to please God (He 11:1ff; 1 Jn 5:4).

3.   MARKETING

"Marketing" is probably an unusual word to use about N.T. evangelism! However, it is appropriate, for it simply refers to the means by which one makes one's product known - in this case, the gospel.

3.1   PREACHING AND TEACHING

We have already seen how preaching and teaching were the fundamental methods used by the early church to make its message known.

In fact, the word kerugma (= preaching) actually came to be used as a synonym for the message itself (see 1 Co 1:21). There does not appear to be any N.T. exception to the use of the spoken word as an integral part of evangelism.

3.2   SIGNS AND WONDERS

Often, but by no means always, miraculous signs and wonders were done by the apostles. So Paul declares that he preached to the Corinthians *"with a demonstration of the Spirit's power"* (1 Co 2:4 - although Acts 18 makes no specific mention of the supernatural), and that from Jerusalem to Illyricum (north-west of Macedonia) he *"fully"* proclaimed the gospel *"by the power of signs and miracles"* (Ro 15:19). Similarly, the writer to the Hebrews points out how the gospel was confirmed by signs and wonders (He 2:4).

The Book of Acts, of course, has many references to signs and wonders. Often, it was these which attracted interest in the message - as did the healing of the lame man at the temple (3:1 ff); the signs and wonders in Jerusalem (5:12 ff); the signs performed by Philip in Samaria (8:6); the signs and wonders of Paul and Barnabas at Iconium (14:3); the *"special"* signs at Ephesus (19:11); and so on.

Clearly, the supernatural was a vital ingredient in "marketing" the gospel in N.T. days!

---

*   **Think Spot**: *What are the implications of this for evangelism today?*

Consider the use of the word "signs" - what does it suggest?

Note, however, two other factors:

First, signs and wonders do not of themselves convince. A miracle happened in Lystra, but Paul was still rejected and stoned there (Ac 14:8-20). Jesus warned about this and pointed out that only faith in the Word of God would change people's lives (Lu 16:31; Jn 5:46-47).

Second, it does not appear that signs and wonders always occurred in N.T. evangelism. We always read of the proclamation of the Word - but not necessarily of miracles. So with the founding of the churches at Caesarea (Ac 10:1 ff), Pisidian Antioch (13:13-52), Thessalonica (17:1-9) and Berea

(17:10 ff), for example, there is no specific mention of the supernatural (apart from baptism in the Spirit).

Certainly, we see no evidence of the supernatural being "used" on occasions like Paul's hearing before the Sanhedrin (Ac 23:1 ff), or his appearances before Felix, Festus, or Agrippa (24:1 ff). The motivation for signs and wonders is always the welfare of the people concerned, never sensationalism, attention-getting for its own sake, or self-aggrandizement.

Note, for instance, how the sovereign grace of God seems to be a factor in supernatural ministry at times (Ac 4:33; 16:25 ff; 19:11), and how signs and wonders "*confirm*" the word (Mk 16:20; He 2:4); that is, they are not an end in themselves.

3.3   THE HOLY SPIRIT

There are examples of evangelists and apostles being specifically directed by the Holy Spirit to go to certain places or to do certain things. So Philip is sent to the eunuch (Ac 8:26), and then caught away by the Spirit (vs. 39); Peter is directed to Cornelius (10:1 ff; 11:12); Paul and Barnabas are sent out by the Spirit (13:1- 4); Paul is prevented by the Spirit from going to Asia and Bithynia (16:6-7), but then has a vision calling him to Macedonia (vs. 9); and so on.

Obviously, when one is led by the Spirit, one can expect fruitfulness. Other methods of preparing the way may not be needed.

On the other hand, however, the Spirit does not always give such revelation. So Paul and Barnabas are sent out initially by the Holy Spirit, but on the second journey, they go simply to see how the churches they founded are getting on (Ac 15:36 ff).

3.4   PERSECUTION

Strangely enough, persecution and opposition were significant factors in the promotion of the gospel.

From the beginning, the antagonism of the Sanhedrin simply served to draw attention to the apostles - as Gamaliel realized it would (Ac 5:34 ff). Imagine the newsworthiness of being taken by soldiers and thrown into prison - and then supernaturally delivered! (4:17 ff; see also 14:19; 16:16 ff; 19:1 ff).

Also, it was persecution that scattered the believers and resulted in the establishing of churches at Antioch, Samaria, etc. (Ac 8:4 ff; 11:19 ff).

This proved to be the continuing pattern well into the third century. Hence Tertullian's renowned statement, *"The blood of the martyrs is the seed of the church"* (Apology, 50).

The worst thing for a church is community indifference: either favor or opposition is more advantageous.

3.5 Other methods of promotion

The N.T. does not give detailed evidence of other methods of "marketing." However, it would be fair to say that the early missioners used every means at their disposal to make the message known.

> * **Think Spot**: *Do you think the apostles would use advertising media today to acquaint people with their message? Why, or why not?*

4. SUMMARY

Obviously, there is no one correct method for planting a church. It will depend very much on the people and place concerned, the cultural environment, the power of the Spirit, etc. The right method is the one that is right for that time and place.

Nevertheless, some factors are universal, as we have seen, especially an unswerving and uncompromising adherence to the preaching of Christ crucified and risen.

(II) THE KINGDOM OF GOD

INTRODUCTION

While I have devoted a great deal of space to the New Testament church, it is interesting to note that Jesus had much more to say about the kingdom! Indeed, according to the gospel records, Jesus only used the word *"church"* on two occasions (Mt 16:18; 18:17), whereas he referred to the kingdom about 135 times!

It is clearly important, then, that we examine what the Bible has to say about the kingdom of God.

First of all, we shall look at an outline of what the New Testament says about the kingdom. Then we shall compare the kingdom and the church.

1. THE NATURE OF THE KINGDOM

1.1 TERMINOLOGY

The terms *kingdom of God ... kingdom of heaven ... kingdom of Christ ... kingdom of the Father,* are all synonymous. Sometimes just the word "kingdom" is used.

This is readily seen by examining the parallel passages in the gospels where different terms are used for the same thing, e.g. Mt 13:11 = Mk 4:11; Mt 3:17 = Mk 1:15. (Note: only Matthew calls it the kingdom of "heaven.")

See also Ep 5:5 where the kingdom is both of Christ and of God (and cp. 1 Co 15:24; Cl 1:13; Re 11:15).

In fact, Christ himself is identified with the kingdom of God. Compare Mk 10:29 and Lu 18:29; Mk 9:1 and Mt 16:28. See also Ac 8:12; 28:31; Re 12:10.

The word "kingdom" has as its underlying meaning "kingship," that is, the being, nature, and state of a king. In this sense, the kingdom (the kingship of God) has always been present. (See Jn 18:36, RSV.)

However, John the Baptist, Jesus, and Jesus' disciples all speak of the kingdom as imminent, as *"at hand,"* and thus, as still to come. See Mt 3:2; 4:12; 10:2; Lu 9:2; Mt 19:23; 16:28. Jesus said it had been *"forcefully advancing"* since John's day (Mt 11:12). Furthermore, people were looking for the kingdom in the days of Jesus (Mk 15:32; Ac 1:6).

Nevertheless, after Pentecost, the apostles refer to the kingdom in the present tense, as being already here (Ro 14:17; 1 Co 4:20; Cl 1:13-18; 4:11). This suggests there is a sense in which the kingdom was actually established at Pentecost, which may well be what Jesus was referring to in Mt 16:28.

1.2   QUALITY

The kingdom was initially (and still is) invisible (Lu 17:21; Jn 18:36), and was evidenced by spiritual characteristics such as deliverance from demons (Mt 12:28); life (Mt 18:9; Mk 9:47); righteousness, joy, peace (Mt 6:33; Ro 14:17); glory (1 Th 2:12); power (Mk 9:1; 1 Co 4:20); grace (He 12:28); knowledge (Mt 23:12; Lu 11:52); authority and salvation (Re 12:100; light (Cl 1:13).

Basically, the kingdom is to be found wherever believers acknowledge Christ as King.

Since the time of Christ, the kingdom has been experiencing mysterious and hidden growth. See the parables of Mt 13, (the wheat and the tares, the mustard seed, the leaven, the net, and so on). However, it will never automatically absorb everyone (Mt 13:30).

To the disciples was given some insight into these mysteries (Mt 13:11; 16:19).

2.   ENTRY INTO THE KINGDOM

Entry into the kingdom is by new birth (Jn 3:3-5).

But it is not a light matter: *"Forceful men lay hold of it"* (Mt 11:12; Lu 16:16).

It must be sought after (Mt 6:33) by those prepared to do God's will (7:21). The kingdom must be prized above all else (Lu 12:32-34; Mt 13:44-46). There must be no turning back (Lu 9:62).

It is for the poor in spirit (Mt 5:3 = Lu 6:20); the persecuted (Mt 5:10); the humble (19:14); the repentant (8:12; 13:38; 21:31); the pure, the moral, and the true worshipers (Ep 5:5); those who have overcome the desires of the flesh (Ga 5:21); the righteous (1 Co 6:9); the called (1 Th 2:20); and those who suffer for Christ (2 Th 1:5). It was intended for Israel, but many others will share in it (Mt 8:11-12; 21:31).

Indeed, it is only *"through many tribulations"* that we enter the kingdom (Ac 14:22). Thus, there is no easy way.

Nevertheless, the kingdom itself is God's gift to his people (Lu 12:32). It is an inheritance (Mt 25:34; 1 Co 15:50; Ja 2:5), to be received by simple faith (Lu 18:17; Mt 19:14).

3.   FINAL ESTABLISHMENT OF THE KINGDOM

The kingdom will be fully and finally established at the end of the age. Jesus taught about this - *"on that day"* not all who claim to be his followers will enter the kingdom (Mt 7:21); but at the close of the age the kingdom will then be obvious (13:43). It will be characterized by eternal life (25:34 and 46). It will be imperishable (1 Co 15:50). It will be open to all followers of Christ as their reward (2 Pe 1:11; 1 Co 15:50; Mt 25:34).

Other references to a future visible kingdom, free from sin and death are - 1 Co 6:9; Ga 5:21; Ep 5:5; 2 Ti 4:18; Ja 2:5; Re 11:15.

Thus, at Christ's coming, the kingdom will be openly and visibly established in purity and power. All other kingdoms will be subject to it, until it is supreme (1 Co 15:25-28; Ex 37:24-28; Zc 14:18-21). Its members will be those who have been born again, and who do God's will.

Thus, just as there are two aspects (present and future) of salvation (1 Pe 1:5), redemption (Ro 8:23), regeneration (Mt 19:28), etc. so there are two of the kingdom. We are saved now, but the fullness of salvation is still to come. So we are in the kingdom now, but the fullness of the kingdom is also still to come.

Chapel of the Ascension on the Mt. of Olives.

4. PARABLES OF THE KINGDOM

Most of Jesus' parables had to do with the kingdom. How often he began his teaching by saying, *"The kingdom of heaven is like ..."* It is important to interpret the parables correctly, without reading too much into them. They are not allegories, in which almost every point has a symbolic meaning, but parables which normally make only one or two basic points.

So when Jesus says that the kingdom is like a treasure (Mt 13:44) or like a householder (20:1) this is the main point to which he wishes to draw our attention: the story simply focuses on this point. So the parable of the virgins, for instance, is basically a warning to prepare for Christ's coming and for the establishment of the kingdom (13:13, 31). That there is no mention of the bride shows that the parable is not meant to be rigidly followed detail by detail (e.g. as a type of the church).

Key thoughts of some parables in Matthew -

Sower (13:1 ff)	Response of people to the "word of the kingdom" (vs. 19).
Wheat & Tares (13:24 ff)	The kingdom exists side by side with evil until the day of the Lord. Christians are "sons of the kingdom" (vs. 38).
Mustard Seed (13:31)	The growth of the kingdom, initially unseen.
Leaven (13:33)	The growth of the kingdom, initially unseen.
Treasure (13:44)	The value of the kingdom.
Pearl (13:45)	The value of the kingdom.
Net (13:47)	As for "Wheat and Tares."
Unjust Servant (18:23)	Forgiveness is a necessary qualification for entrance into the kingdom.
Vineyard (20:1)	All are treated equally in the kingdom.
Marriage Feast (22:2)	The invitation is to both Jews and Gentiles, but all alike need to be clothed in God's righteousness.
Virgins (25:1)	Readiness for the day of the Lord and the establishment of the kingdom.

5.   WHAT IS THE DIFFERENCE

The essential difference between the church and the kingdom is really fairly simple. The church is fully realized here and now whereas the kingdom is not. As we have seen, the word "church" means literally an "assembly" or "meeting together" of God's people: it is a present, visible manifestation of Christ. The kingdom, on the other hand, is not yet fully manifested.

Basically, the same people are involved in each, of course. Certainly, the same strict requirements of righteousness are enjoined upon members of both kingdom and church. Entry into both kingdom and church is the same - repentance, faith, new birth (Mt 4:17; 18:3; Ac 2:38, 47; Jn 3:5; 1 Pe 1:3; 1 Jn 2:29; 5:1; etc.).

Yet there is a subtle difference. The church is the assembly of God's people meeting together as a body; the kingdom is the rule of God in the hearts of his people. One is visible; the other invisible. Hence, churches may be openly afflicted by disunity - it is easy for a "visible" organization to be divided up and each part "labeled." Because the kingdom is invisible, however, it is indivisible. There is only ever one King; all of his subjects belong to but one kingdom.

> *   **Think Spot**: *"No N.T. apostle or evangelist ever preached the church; they always preached the kingdom." Is that valid? If so, what are the implications for today? Is it possible to be in the kingdom, but not the church (or vice versa?). Would a reversal to the N.T. preaching emphasis help to promote greater unity in the church today?*

6.   CONCLUSION

The kingdom of God is now in existence wherever people own him as King. On the day of the Lord, the kingdom will be manifested in power. All believers will share in it. It will be supreme over all other kingdoms. *"And the earth will be filled with the knowledge of the glory of the Lord as the waters cover the sea"* (Ha 2:14).

Meanwhile, the true subjects of the kingdom meet together in assembly for worship, fellowship and teaching - and this meeting together is in its truest sense the church.

BIBLIOGRAPHY

Recommended texts -

    HARPER, Michael; *Let My People Grow* (Hodder, 1977)

    SAUCY, Robert; *The Church in God's Program* (Moody, 1972)

Recommended reading -

    BANKS, Robert; *Paul's Idea of Community* (Anzea, 1979)

    BERKOUWER, G. C.; *The Church* (Eerdmans, 1976)

    GETZ, Gene; *Sharpening the Focus of the Church* (Moody, 1974)

    MOYES, Gordon; *How to Grow an Australian Church* (Vital, 1975)

    RADMACHER, Earl; *What the Church is All About* (Moody, 1978)

    SNYDER, Howard; *The Problem of Wineskins* (IVP, 1977)

Reference books -

    BERKHOF, Louis; *The New International Dictionary of New Testament Theology* (Zondervan, 1979)

    BRUCE, F. F.; *The Book of Acts* (Eerdmans, 1973)

    CALVIN, John; *The Institutes of the Christian Religion* (James Clarke & Co. 1962)

    HASTINGS, James (ed.); *Dictionary of the Bible*

    KITTEL, Gerhard; *Theological Dictionary of the N.T.*

    MOULTON & MILLIGAN; *The Vocabulary of the Greek New Testament* (Hodder, 1963)

    UNGER, M.; *Unger's Bible Dictionary* (Moody, 1957)

Background reading -

    AUGUSTINE; *City of God*

    EDERSHEIM, Alfred; *The Life and Times of Jesus the Messiah* (MacDonald)

    EUSEBIUS; *History of the Church* (Penguin, 1965)

JOSEPHUS; *Complete Works* (Kregel, 1969)

ROBERTS & DONALDSON (ed.); *The Ante-Nicene Fathers* (Eerdmans, 1979)

STANIFORTH, Maxwell (ed.); *Early Christian Writings* (Penguin, 1968)

Commentaries, Lexicons, etc. -

Various commentaries, lexicons, histories, etc., were drawn upon in the writing of this series of lessons.

www.ingramcontent.com/pod-product-compliance
Lightning Source LLC
Chambersburg PA
CBHW022051050726
47591CB00002B/489